MIND, LIFE & *Reflections*

Payal Jain

Invincible Publishers

First published in India in 2018

ISBN: 978-93-88333-25-2

Invincible Publishers

G-120, Sushant Lok III, Sector 57, Gurgaon-122002

Registered Address: Opposite Kasturba Ashram,
Radaur, Haryana–135133

Printed in India by Excel Printers Pvt. Ltd.

You are a door

To pass through lessons always

So until the sun finally sets its blazing rays

And as this door witnesses goings and comings

Remember these would be moments defining your being

-PaYal

Life, Thank You For Everything

Thank you! Life
For always heading forward even with hurdles,
For keeping my faith intact,
though I strayed at times with distrust,
For never giving up on me even when my belief was shaken,
For pouring me with the love of family and friends,
For showing me miracles that followed the hard times,
For serving me with reasons to get up everyday,
For giving me strength through ups and lows,
For countless experiences that complete me for sure,
For giving me people to look up to,
For giving me the scars and making me resilient,
Thank you for completing me in many ways...
For filling me with life and giving me
existence through the lessons.

Foreword

A ninth standard girl, tom boyish, excellent at table tennis, a poetess with clarity of thought with power pounding words, ready to conquer the world...

An eleventh standard girl, reader of heavy philosophy, dropping quotes while engaging her friends amidst endless laughter behind the steering wheel, ready to take on the world in her single stride...

A feminine, graceful woman, a blend of modernity and ethnicity, a wife, a mother, a daughter, a daughter in law...

A social worker, an entrepreneur, a life coach, a mentor, a friend... and now a writer of the Book: Mind, Life & Reflections.

All these rolled into one is Payal Jain, a friend and a role model, as I have known her for the past 30 years to see a girl become a lady and a woman of substance bringing joy to the people around her, be it at home or at the orphanages she visits, bringing structure and character to the many businesses she started and handed over for people to run, bringing hope and creating pathways for countless many whose lives she touched as a life coach. This book has been penned down when she was at the Zenith of her career and personal accomplishments defined in the realms of love, family values and peace of mind. Payal has drawn a lot in life from scriptures and philosophy. Bhagwad Gita is a bed side book for her. Bible has helped her for drawing parallels and reinforcements. In addition she has read Osho, excerpts from Upanishads and believes in God for clinging, turning back, leaning on to for support.

A heart of gold yet grit and determination in will and action define her work with words over 30 chapters exuding feelings and thoughts creating reading time and space for any reader thirsting for being able to relate with a blend of life philosophy, reasons to the explainable, the challenge to accept the unexplainable and ability to discover the conquering force within. The book continuously unleashes the dormant energy within to recognise self-worth and take a step forward, unhindered, and untamed to rise to your full potential at every turn of events in your life.

This book, Mind, Life & Reflections, comes as a poetic expression from her pen as she transformed her pain, of losing her mother at an early age, to creative energies of nurturing others' lives. It may have been a tearing, seething pain veiled by smiles worn like a fortitude of fortress of strength gathered from life experiences, where breaking down was acceptable momentarily. The book repeatedly leads you to stand tall, gathering strength by learning life's lessons from circumstances, everyday events and seeing reason in every human interaction and a continuous leaning on God.

Each chapter opens with a poetic expression that strums a deep emotion with the reader engaging him / her emotionally and intellectually. Each poem is followed by a narrative which brings up life events which builds up a strong reader-writer connect. The play of words throughout the poem and the narrative carries the reader through his own life journey as he draws semblance with his own heart-mind-soul journey in this lifetime.

The chapters flow like bead to bead as if in a string of life, with each bead encapsulating a thought, a phase , a lesson learnt like that of a maala-jap bead to bead progression. Yet at places the chapters offer a surprising contrast to the previous one playing with elevations and dips or troughs of emotions beautifully wafered to keep the interest alive.

The book has a natural expression at times bringing in notes from psychologists, poets like Shakespeare, religious texts etc and at times Hindi poetic verses written by her at different occasions. This lacing and interspersing narrative forms a free flowing connect which is boundary-less. It is a book on self-discovery in an easy language, kindling the thought and lighting fire within. It will bring easy solutions and one may find help on unresolved issues. It may be a good idea to sit with a pencil or mark lines with highlighter as you enjoy the book or you may find yourself clicking images from books to refer to friends on social media!!

I loved every word, every line and the message between the lines.

Lt. Cdr(retd.) Vibhuti Gupta

Associate Director, ZIKR

Delhi

[illegible] playing [illegible] and dips [illegible] the humanity watered to keep the [illegible]

The book has a natural expression at times [illegible] quotes [illegible] poets like Shakespeare, [illegible] Hindi poets [illegible] The loving and [illegible] which [illegible] a journey of self-discovery [illegible] thought and [illegible] [illegible]

[illegible]

[illegible]

[illegible]

Delhi

Introduction

One fine day in August 2018, on a morning just like any other of my schedule that starts at 4.30 AM, I was taking a jog in the park. All of a sudden, a bolt of lightning lit up the park whilst the park lights went off due to some electric circuit botch. Thunder and more lightning followed with a heavy rain shower that drenching me down while I kept jogging. Rain poured down my face and I was soaked from head to toe, not only with raindrops but also with an image so clear and vivid that of a book cover with a title 'Mind, Life & Reflections'.

The rain continued to pour, while the wind, now settled, did laps matching up to my jogging pace round the darkened path. The raindrops landing on my face felt so contenting, making me feel life run through me, holding me in that moment. Looking around, I realised how rain just pours and runs into whatever comes in its way, creating a multiplicity of sounds by bumping into a myriad of elements and playing an orchestrated poetic performance. That moment when the rain was pouring on me captivating me with the sounds of life that I have heard all this while; the chirpy sounds of a carefree childhood, the thumping sounds of dreams, the sobbing sounds from a wounded self, the pleasant melodious sounds of first love, the screeching sounds from matters of convenience, the nagging sounds of procrastination, the weeping sounds of changed friendships, the sulking sounds of regrets, and so many more.

From birth to death, we all go through a series of emotions, breakthroughs and transformations that uphold our way of 'being in the world'. Some try to fit in with the world while masking their true selves the whole time they are here, while others make their own mark, leaving a trail when they leave. All of us learn lessons in many ways throughout, even though we realise some of these lessons and some we don't. Regardless, we will find out some day why it happened the way it did, but till then we all will continue experiencing our meant-to-be lessons; living through our lives.

Life is very much like a poem with verses of different emotions that make us happy, sad, hurt, loved and so much more. Yet, without any one of these experiences or emotions, the puzzle of our life would simply be incomplete, not sounding like the orchestrated poetic performance, for a note would be missing. When the pieces of the puzzle are complete as we feel and comprehend, everything just starts making sense from the beginning till the end. We all are poets of our lives, making verses of our experiences, seeking the truth of our existence. Some express it through words, some through other art forms, and others still do it in their own ways to reach out to the world.

'Mind, Life & Reflections' may jolt you or concoct stillness in you with questions like; do you run your life or your life is running you? Are you doing what is required or what you are meant to do? Are you in charge or the charge is in hands of what life throws? Are you sinking down with the ups and downs or you choose to grow?

'Mind, Life & Reflections' is about the emotions we feel in our expressions, the experiences of life, and how the same reflect on us, shadowing or revealing our true selves and giving meaning to our existence. This book will linger on with you, taking you on to a roller- coaster of such emotions and experiences, riding, moving, exposing and contemplating your perspective that may change your life forever.

The First Lesson

Life turns to another time and I, the soul, returns,
In the mother's womb safe, all curled, while ma yearns…
This beautiful journey of patience and endurance,
Firmly instilling purpose and perseverance…
Trusting in God's sanctification and his plan set right,
Blood running through my veins, this is home with no light…
Yet feels like the safest place to be in on this entire earth,
My nourishing known heaven for months of hope and warmth…

Dipped in the simplest and the most complex reality splash,
Knitting as a child how world became flesh in a flash…
The inviolability of the life growing inside ma overwhelms her new days,
Making ma sacrifice comfort in unique ways…
Doubts sometimes visiting my safest paradise,
Putting in pictures of the unknown on the other side…
Embryonic tiny toes come to be with fast time ticking,
Scared by the changes and so the kicking…

With passing time, I am concocting perceptions of an unfamiliar realm,

Slowly steps in fear and anxiety, coming out of the confine whelms…

Comfort finds its way and walks along in ma's soothing voice,

'My water broke', and my world is upside down with that noise…

As I cling on frightened, longing to stay safer and embrace what I know,

Ma puts her body through its most strenuous test; I am struggling to let it go…!

Amidst all that pain and pool of blood between ma's thighs,

I manage through the tiny passage, much to my surprise…

Born as a warrior, defying odds and winning the most petrifying battles of all,

Narrow or wide, the only margin walls that ever existed were in my mind, shouted the call...

My jubilant ma felt the most amazing and miraculous thing in the world and took the side,

Feeling like an erudite, I learnt my first lesson; life won't be an easy ride…

Always remember that obstacles only exist because you conceive,

Don't you ever forget this and despite all, you did achieve.

-PaYal Jain

Not On An Easy Ride

Much has been spoken about the mother, a woman whose body becomes a living sacrifice for her child in many ways. From keeping her child safe in the womb, to giving birth from between her thighs, she joins the pedigree of multitudinous women who relinquish and let go of so much in the wake of motherhood. Delivering a baby naturally is incredibly powerful and also overwhelms a woman, being completely at the mercy of nature. When you face that type of pain, you have to be exceptionally committed; committed to bring the life inside to a safe delivery of your child into the world outside, while you put all your trust into your remarkable body and let it take over and do what it naturally knows what to do. Likewise, the life inside just knows what to do to come out of that tiny passage to embark on the journey, joining the human race.

As the mother goes into labour and experiences light contractions, considerably minutes apart until they're every five minutes, the life inside must feel a little scared, a little curious and topsy turvy on the whole. Surely that explains the woman's body producing lots of oxytocin during labour, which puts the baby in a content and calm mood. Light contractions are replaced by powerful ones, making the life inside feel a bit squashed and uncomfortable for slight moments, and with less oxygen too, only to realise later the creation of a super power to cope with this. The super power may surprise the life inside on beating the walls that are caving in on it while being helped by the mother who gives the child all the air it needs to breathe before exploring the unexplored.

The mother lies on her back and focuses on pushing the baby down the birth canal, whilst the life inside prepares for its first ride through that narrow passage. The ride is not an easy one for sure and also not an impossible one, equipped with the most effective tools of mother nature, fitting just right through an opening roughly the diameter of a bagel. These effective tools make the baby press its head into the birth canal and stagger with the job at hand. Because of the efficient contrivances placed right, like the flexible skull plates, the dilation position and so on, the baby is taken aback by its own remarkable natural ability to mould into the shape of the birth canal as it journeys through it. That explains the cone head that some babies are born with, though it returns to normal within a few days. The moment the newly born cone head is able to pull the entire being into the new space, defeating the fears and worries of the uncertainties and anxiety of the unknown, the life once inside now cries out. It is a shout out to the world that despite all odds, I overcame my limiting beliefs, my fears and I won.

While the umbilical cord is clamped, shutting the placenta out of its job, the lungs of this little life expand with pride and fill with air, while the heart, already in action, pumps more blood through them. Science is yet to define the exact pain felt by a baby while it squeezes through the tight space, establishing facts regarding the baby's auditory and visual skills. Science continues its journey on reconnoitering a baby's feelings during those nine months and then travelling through the birth canal.

We all have been there, taken the path from the known to the unknown, handling it in our own way. A few may have also suffered broken collar bones or shoulder dystocia in the birth canal to prove their strength and victory. We all have been squished and had our skulls elongated to get through that narrow uncomfortable passage, then announced with a cry that regardless of the unknown new, we substantiated and confirmed our beliefs in our own strengths to come up and conquer the unknown. The stay in the womb may have been safe, but there were times certainly which brought on a desire for knowledge of the other side till we were ready to face the fear.

All of us take our own time to leave our safe known world to move to the world unknown and beyond the womb to the worldly realms. The reason for the same is God's own plans and the timing for us to be ready. It is never early, and it's never late. It is just when we are ready, we will face what is meant to be. We come to the world and learn our first lesson in the process. We must remind ourselves of it whenever we are struggling with the where, when, what and how. That is the time to hark back to the unknown, which may have been terrifying, but is reminiscent of our strengths and God's plan.

Many of us cling to our fears or doubts, for there is an undeniable sanctuary in the known, even if it resides in the corner of our darkest familiar pains. It seems a lot safer to hold on to what we have a knowledge of, than to face the unknown. Just as when we were born, we might have thought we were dying, afraid of the unknown without realising that the death was just another birth: just a transition and a victory.

Break The Conflicted Vision Wall

Perfectly hidden, I the soul often think, "Who am I?"
Musing feelings in feelings, I sigh!
Watching me come out of ma's womb to the universe,
'It is a fair looking girl,' announced the nurse;
Another edition bolstering the kin cable
Born fair into a Hindu family was then my label…

Ever since, I have been vacuum packed in a fallacy box;
Suffocated with all prejudicial parameters, turning myself into a corpse,
Chained in ignorance, forced and coerced by the world that formulated me
Fooling myself while chasing the mirage, seeing what others did see
Isn't it funny that when I took birth and cried, other babies did the same?
We were meant to connect like always and not play the pull down label game…

Once in a while, put yourself off the pedestal, freeing yourself from the perfection blend

Seek the real you, rip off the labels and bring to light that for which you were sent

Time to end the conflict within is now; rejuvenate each day,

Time to rise above the friction around and say our say

Break out from the shell of conflicted vision,

A liberated butterfly; a beautiful creation

Spread your wings out, you were meant to be free;

Listen carefully to your inner voice and heed to the plea

Stop fitting into slots and explore the *You Unlimited*;

Removing all labels, walking away from the rigid

No more living at the mercy of a reasoning so small

Acknowledge who you truly are and just stand tall.

-PaYal Jain

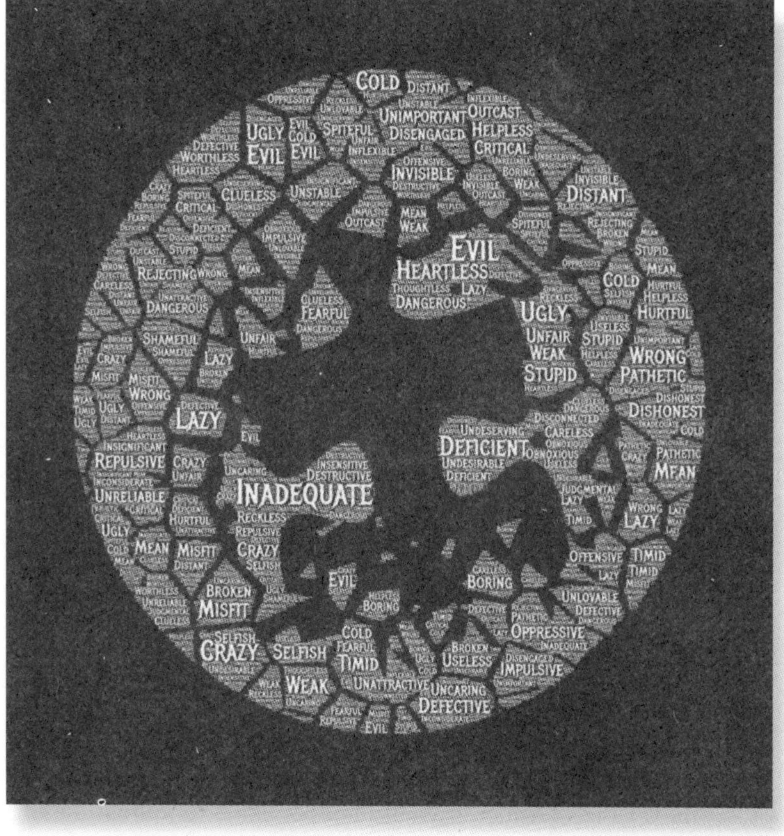
COLD
DISTANT
UNIMPORTANT
OUTCAST
UGLY
SPITEFUL
DISENGAGED
HELPLESS
WORTHLESS
EVIL
CRITICAL
INVISIBLE
CLUELESS
UNSTABLE
DISTANT
MEAN
WEAK
EVIL
HEARTLESS
DANGEROUS
REJECTING
FEARFUL
UGLY
UNFAIR
WEAK
STUPID
WRONG
PATHETIC
SHAMEFUL
LAZY
DISHONEST
DEFICIENT
REPULSIVE
INADEQUATE
MEAN
UNRELIABLE
RECKLESS
CRAZY
LAZY
MISFIT
TIMID
OFFENSIVE
BORING
BROKEN
MISFIT
UNLOVABLE
DEFECTIVE
OPPRESSIVE
CRAZY
SELFISH
TIMID
USELESS
IMPULSIVE
WEAK
UNATTRACTIVE
UNCARING
DEFECTIVE
EVIL

The Labels

Are you a successful person or do you consider yourself a loser? Does the world see you as sexy or are you just too fat? Are you efficient enough or a good-for-nothing? Does the world eye you in scrutiny because you belong to a particular race and religion? Do you fall on the good side or the 'other' side of the society? Are you considered abnormal because the world does not swing by your sexual preferences? Are you making enough money to be tagged as rich, or are you on the poor pitch? Are you religious, doing your rituals right, or just an atheist questioning existence all the time?

What labels have been given to you by the world and what labels have you attached to yourself lately, believing that they define you. Confining identities to categorical boxes–religious or spiritual, social, political, economic and others–may have facilitated in putting an end to the unmanageable intricacies of the diverse world we live in, but has contributed to butchering the uniqueness of our being.

We are surely not defined by just one thing, but are an amalgamation of many infinitesimal forces consolidated in the heterogeneity of habitation conventions, cultures and identities. These categories are like a bewildering set of boxes out of which it would not be viable to journal the information on our minds during our lives. No one can deny the enduring stabilities of these concerns, but there seems no reason except fear and prejudice to keep acting on the same, bursting at the seams, as if this was all that human life was all about.

When you were in your mother's womb, were you black or white? You came out and were given your first appearance based identity which the world was taught to say of you. What's more, with another set of nuances for other countless compartments to put you in, the world created a plastic identity for you, a sheer mockery of reality to the extent that you failed recognising yourself as you every time. Did you ever question yourself deep down, or catechized who you really were? Or did you just carry the voluminous baggage of tags and labels along, believing them all to be you? If you actually dig through the pages of history, you would know that the concept of differentiation on the basis of race was invented just some centuries ago. All this while, the genesis of the concept of race and its contribution towards wiping away the truth of one's being, concealing one's true identity, revealing the man-made tags and labels has worked perfectly well.

Alan R. Templeton, Ph.D., Professor of Biology in Arts and Sciences at Washington University, says, "Race is a real cultural, political and economic concept in society, but it is not a biological concept, and that unfortunately is what many people wrongfully consider to be the essence of race in humans–genetic differences."

Over the past few decades, a fair amount of genetic research has taken place globally, analysing the DNA of global human populations. Science has concluded that we are all mixed up genetically, edifying deep truths about our roots. The moment we are born, the label voyage embarks, even though no one is born with them. Walk through the corridors of a hospital and gaze through the windows of the nurseries for new-borns; you will notice that when one new-born cries, all the babies start crying like-wise. It elucidates that no-matter what the gender, culture, caste, creed, colour or other labels one is assigned may be, we are meant to connect without the filter of labels, while being kind and giving, proliferating love and care for each other.

Did it ever occur to you why we play the label game? Take a moment to cogitate and ponder over the forceful veracity built around the unnecessary labels. The process speaks of our own convoluted, contradictory and sometimes evolving nature. Placing labels on others or even yourself is like taking the easier road with minimum pits and falls. It gives a seemingly safer route to traverse on with comrades or antagonists in life. For sure, the alternate choice requires a lot more effort.

Maybe it is time to ask yourself whether you are comfortable in your own skin? Go ahead and do that right now, then explain the unnerving feeling you just experienced. We may take pride in our strengths but in speaking of our weaknesses…I might have touched the wrong chord there. Have you never come across a religious head who fulminates over same sex connubial unions, and then is caught in flagrante delicto with his gay partner? Are you not reminded here of iconic celebrities who protest against all sorts of treachery, but are then exposed for the same negative traits on surreptitious news channels.

Judging a person is hard, knowing a person is harder, and understanding a person is the hardest.

That's the reason we go on judging others and ourselves. It's comforting and convenient to identify and relate. It is a habit and a contagious one too. We shell ourselves in fearing hurt, and save our real selves from pain by hiding under cloaks of sham. It is also convenient to locate other members of "our tribe" with these labels. We have all fallen prey to such conditioning, for the way this world feeds us this phony attribute from the moment we are born. Think about your first math lesson. "This is one. This is two." And we learn distinct categories. Consider this categorical labelling via this analogy. You have a library in your mind. This library sorts books of information and places them in different sections, so that when you need to find a particular book, you just know where to look. It aids an individual's cognition, but also leads the way to stereotyping. "It wears a dress and has long hair. Aha! It must be a girl. If it is a girl, then it must not roam alone on roads at night!"

Girl child of the human race! What good fortune has a horse undressed of its saddle, with a mane of hair, yet free to roam on untagged pastures, no labels, no titles, no gene of the human race!

Knowingly or unknowingly, we put ourselves in pre-defined and confining boxes, trying to set down our delineation. We put labels on ourselves as well as others. Whether positive or negative, what we divulge to our minds each day holds the power to dictate the direction of our thoughts and actions. The labels we attach to ourselves can be powerful motivators or detractors. Where the label has come from, whether from the world around or self- arbitration, it doesn't matter.

If you adopt, reinforce, and feed the label in your mind – you are simply giving it power over you.

Being aware is the first step towards ending the conflict within. Challenge the label before it challenges you and take the reins of your life, the baton on your actions, in your own hands. Is the label a veracity that can't be changed, or is it just your interpretation? Gather yourself up. You may have failed, but do you plainly believe in *once a failure, always a failure?* You can change that good for nothing feeling, learn from your mistakes and try again and again till you succeed. You can do without the label of a loser and remember, a winner is just a loser who tried one more time.

There are some things that are beyond our control. Maybe you had an accident, lost a limb. Maybe you were born with a disability. That's not something that you asked for, or was caused deliberately by you, so simply stop letting it define you. You are as blind, as weak, as stupid, etc. as you choose to be. To err is human, we all make mistakes. Let one moment not define or judge you. Speaking of judging, it is like a tool for proving ourselves over and over again, wherein defining others with these labels outlines the peripheries of our astuteness.

She is with a new guy every day. She is a whore.

Do you know she speaks rubbish all the time? She is stupid.

Look at his breast. He is the plus size nerd.

People will judge you whether you like it or not, and they will do it before you judge them, always a step up in the label game–thinking themselves to be great analysts and jumping to conclusions too soon. Does it really matter? There is no point in comparing someone's chapter ten with your chapter one. Don't let these conclusions, these labels, become your reality. Whether you change them or let them be as they are, you always have the choice to act upon them at any given point of time.

All of us are competent enough for concrete authentic change, but we often feel too terrified to break the shell of conflicted visions, making the real appear blurred. Labels play with our mind, successfully undermining our unprecedented authentic self. But don't we all long at some point in our lives to break free of all the labels and be our true selves in the most genuine way possible? Don't we long to be in a relationship with life, rather than with expectations rising out of these labels? Don't we all want to break free and fly away from these artificial filters keeping us from truly being who we are meant to be? Each one of us is exceptional and unique, but we have forgotten this, blinded by the labels and made ignorant of our special qualities within.

To do or not to do, to be or not to be, to be chained or to break free, to be in the box or out of it, there will always be a choice, and availing it is always your call without the prejudice of right or wrong. Choose well of the two.

Chained in labels or standing tall, breaking the labels' walls?

Bring Back The Carefree Child

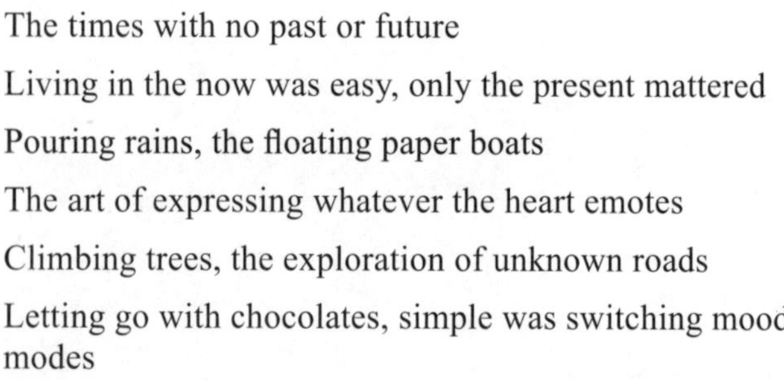

The times with no past or future
Living in the now was easy, only the present mattered
Pouring rains, the floating paper boats
The art of expressing whatever the heart emotes
Climbing trees, the exploration of unknown roads
Letting go with chocolates, simple was switching mood modes
Having mischiefs up on our sleeves was the fashion code
Bring those smiles from the carefree childhood, the heavenly abode.

Not giving up on anything till the victorious smile
Embarrassment did not shame the face, only trying mattered
Scribbling with crayons till pleased with masterpieces
The never ending questions coming from learning caprices
Happiness is then what cricket or other sports teach
Imagination went wild with wonder-knitting dreams
Faith ruled, coupled with endless schemes
Bring gleams from the carefree childhood, the heavenly stream.

Masks of superheroes or cartoons worn at birthday parties
Always caught up in the act of camouflage, only veracity mattered
The extra inches did not bother around the waist
Confidence did not die by the brands or my watch's rate
Everything was said and done, no holding on to grudges' plate
Saying NO when I needed to, genuinely living all my emotion parades
Living with utter arbitrariness, nothing could make me afraid
Bring candour from the carefree childhood, the heavenly arcade.

Here, like a little child I stand
Searching for the inner child on a grown person's land
While the child within tries to hold on
Chaos takes over, saying your time is gone
For childhood nostalgia does hit me at times
Slaying the child in life's churn feels like a crime
Voices in my head randomly pass through
Calling for me to keep the child alive in you

- PaYal Jain

The Lost Childhood

The little girl or boy within each one of us needs to be cherished. That adept being who was once capable of doing anything is now repressed under layers of responsibilities, and needs some nourishment. Remember, when you were a little kid, you did not worry about the dirt on your shoes, the stains on your clothes, or how your face looked. You just wanted to get drenched in the rains, float paper boats, run through the puddle and create a splash, climb trees and pluck the fruits, or just paint your face with your new-found love for water colours. You climbed up that hill many a times without feeling tired, as the thrill to race down and feel the cool breeze on your face inspired you. You have done all that and so much more when life was just a playground and everything was fun, when you were a carefree child once upon a time. There is a child inside each one of us who wants to have fun, come out once in a while and feel life as a playground again, without worrying our pretty little heads about winning or losing the game.

Childhood remains one of the greatest psychological mysteries of all times. Babies and young children are armed with amazing learning abilities. A research by Alison Gopnik, a PhD psychologist from the University of California at Berkeley, suggests that very young children can and do understand the perspectives of others, and that their thinking about other people changes as they learn more about the world and themselves. Her findings enunciate that harnessing the thinking behind such irrationalities, as a 3-year-old's wild make-believe, may help adults write novels, invent new technologies and plan for a better future.

Simple things such as blowing bubbles that excited and fascinated you once, are now considered immature or are used as shallow gimmicks for Instagram posts. We oscillate between getting stressed or elated, dependent on other's reactions on our social media timelines. We constantly doubt and question ourselves, just because our bubble picture may not be in vogue with the trending posts. We choose not to live the experience of blowing bubbles, indulge in the innocent fun of the activity and take delight in its beauty, but are fixated with showing off our perfect filtered shots, for the sake of pretending to the whole world that your are happy with your perfect bubble.

For reasons best known to ourselves, we grownups are fixated on making things happen and completely weeding out everything else beyond that. But look at the carefree child, not quite adept at maintaining focus on one thing, but taking in new ideas that come from the unexpected events. They may not be the best planners in the world, but try to beat them when it comes to creativity and discovery. These carefree children can give you the best solutions to mind-numbing issues and unleash an ocean of possibilities. Go to the park and see these carefree children playing. They possess a fearless demeanour, climbing the tallest of trees. Even falling several times does not stop them; they are completely unaffected by the falling experience!

It has gotten me to think many a times, *what changes?* What is it that manages to lock the carefree childhood somewhere, hiding the curious, direct, inquisitive, and creative child? Over the years, the child within is slayed under the pressure of expectations to excel at everything, be involved in the education system of our schools, forcibly participate in dull extracurriculars, etc., to eventually join the rat race to please or appease their parents and their buried desires and pleasures. The carefree child then dance to the manipulating tunes of the times, bidding goodbye to his carefree childhood.

The carefree child once spoke her heart out, then discovered the judgements. There were times when people around picked holes in her feelings and taught her to behave in a certain manner. This newly introduced fear of rejection worked to manipulate and contradict her natural feelings and actions. She started to act in palpable modes meant to placate others, including her parents, her peers, her friends, and just about everyone she knew. In other words, she detested it, but still wore masks of pretence, shooing away the child who used to fight over the choice of masks to be worn at birthday parties. As grownups, we have so many masks at our disposal, customised corresponding to the state of play and circumstances we are in.

Science explains the difference in brain development and learning capacity between children and adults, enabling the child's brain to be able to learn nearly anything and everything, while the picture is quite the other way for adults. Children are born in the sizes they are to survive childbirth, making them completely helpless, unlike several other species where the newly born can use their limbs immediately after birth. A child's brain is constantly growing, so learning becomes a naturally enjoyable phenomena. Besides the scientific rationalization, children are carefree because they are not introduced to the set patterns of life yet. These set parameters make us worry about our performance as adults, making us forget to relax, laugh and be truly happy, living life in the moment, completely untouched by demands of the future or the scars of the past.

The little child inside of us is hiding somewhere underneath layers of charade, wanting to be out with long kept secrets, his locked dreams and desires. As we grow up, we lose the connection with that carefree child and look for sources outside of us for pleasure or inspiration. In the quest to fill that void within, we push the inner child deeper, burying it in layers. Don't let that child suffocate and eventually die. Growing up is natural, so we should enjoy the changes we undergo. I remember when I used to fantasise about growing up, I actually wished to be inside the TV box while a secret magic wand turned me into an adult endorsed to do anything.

Willingly or unwillingly, we all grow up, and this change is not only inevitable, but a very significant one too. As adults, we are more independent to explore the various aspects of life, but often lose the zeal and the enthusiasm to accept new things and ideas. We are so tied up with our set opinions, changing our perspective about things and our thoughts become very difficult. Unlike the carefree child, our egos stand to get hurt in adulthood.

As adults, we accept the way things are around us and don't concern ourselves with change. Despite having enough strength, we don't ask questions like a carefree child. We are victims of routine and complacency, dwelling more upon the ifs and buts instead of having faith in our guts. We all are born creative, but lose our 'originality' over time to the conditioning of our society and the labels fed to us by the world. Don't let this superpower of your inner child be compromised as you grow up. Keep going with a never give up attitude.

Keep this child alive and it'll help you push your way through life. The more in harmony we are with this inner child, the more blissfully we sail through life. Stay young by keeping the child within happy, sprightly and kicking. Enjoy the small things, laugh, run around without a care in the world, solve puzzles, learn a musical instrument, paint, have that pastry you have been salivating on without stressing over the calories. Never say, "I'm too old for this," and embrace the carefree child within you.

Oh my lost childhood
Visit me once in a while
Carefree spirit to touch me again
The puddling, the rowing paper boats in the rain
Wish to turn back the wheels of time
That does not seems to be possible
Oh my carefree childhood visit me once in a while
Want to be upset while the world conspiring to make me smile
And then fill myself with joy seeing the pampering and the gift pile
Not bothered with who said what with no agenda to follow
No egos, grudges or pride to swallow
Free me from the worldly deceptions
Oh my carefree childhood visit me once in a while
Sitting with masks of deception
Grown up with justifications and this child's destruction
Waiting for the meet up one more time
Oh my carefree childhood visit me once in a while

Pain Or Freedom?

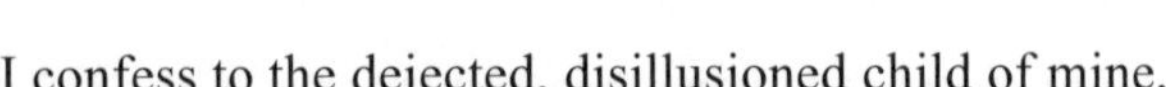

I confess to the dejected, disillusioned child of mine,
For I have kept you locked for too long, thinking I'd be fine...
If only I could reach in and say sorry
For the times when violence, neglect and betrayal knocked;
For the times when early sex came with pain, disgust and shock;
For the times when you encountered sudden death of a closed one;
For the times I betrayed you and chose to run…

If only I could reach in and say sorry
For I did not gather the courage to look for you;
For I abandoned you while a defensive me was rising anew;
For I chose to close my ears to the cries inside;

If only I could reach in and say sorry
For suffocating you in walls so thick and cold;
For shutting you out in the process of being bold;
For keeping you, my sweet child, in persistent pain;
For letting the deep rooted scars remain;

As I confess, I see the wounded child pass by

It's okay! I love you, sobbing I said in a sigh,

'Sorry,' I said, complying with my child, bringing her near;

Smiling, she patted me for confronting my fear,

It turned out fine by telling the wounded child, *I'm here to stay;*

For I chose the final freedom when persistent pain came to play.

\- **PaYal Jain**

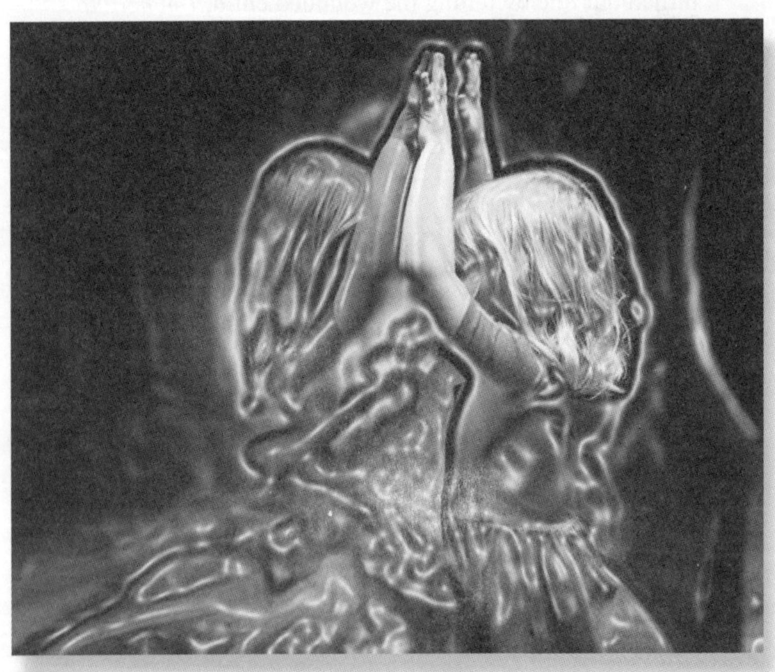

I Am Sorry, 'My Wounded Child'

When the scars are deep and the healing is shallow, the echo of wounds remains for a lifetime. We are hurt and crushed and suppress the wounds deep down, experiencing relinquishment. We are haunted all the while with "What's wrong with me?" In children, the inner self is naïve and vulnerable, and the wounds induced by physical abuse, violence, prolonged neglect, sudden death of a closed one, violations and others clout the coping mechanism, resulting in one building sturdy defence walls around, shutting the chances of being wounded ever again. But we forget that putting the bandage outside with work, alcohol, recreational treats and other things do not stop the bleeding inside. It will only stop when we gather our strength and deal with the core, and make peace with it.

Childhood is not always a pretty picture and the scars of childhood can remain throughout our lives, as these wounds are engraved on every cell of our body. Trauma encountered at a time when we were meant to be safe and happy brings instability, insecurity, and other tormenting experiences well into your adult life. The brutal truth of the trauma suffered can nail you apart and weigh you down time and again, and dealing with the beleaguered is the only way out. The scars and the wounds, regardless of their profundity, do not imply a life sentence that sways all the life force in you.

"A wound is the place where the light enters you." – Rumi

Some days, we just feel down and depressed, blemished by the blood of our souls' wounds–ones that never saw the light, that were denied or ignored, locked inside a closet hidden from everyone, and eventually forgotten. Yet they come back to confuse us from time to time when our agony is triggered. No medicine helps in getting permanently rid of this continuous throbbing pain. Binging on food, going over the top with partying or on a shopping spree may fix it for a day or a few, but you will continue to feel a void–a space that spells nothingness–until you put those broken pieces back together.

We all have felt unworthy, undefinable, incomprehensible at some point of our lives, not deserving of happiness, delectation, or love. Even if these beliefs are coming from substantial juvenile anguishes akin to physical, sexual, or psychological abuse, they will continue to impact, control and contribute to deep mental and emotional patterns that drive your thoughts, feelings and actions while you are battling inside about changing or fixing something about yourself in order to be acceptable.

Have you ever felt an unexplained surge of anxiety, anger or any other strong emotion occurring consistently? Does it make you wonder about the advent of this tempestuous nature in you? Could it be a trigger where wounds from the past try to stick their oar in the present, without a justification or even a warning? Most times through our lives, we may not even know that we are being triggered. These triggers are signs that it's time to heal the wound that is frightened to bare the layers of fear, shame and victimhood, and continues to surround itself with our defence mechanisms.

The feeling of "I am not enough", "I am incomplete", "I am unlovable,", "I don't matter", "I am weak", and "I don't deserve…" incessantly bury you in rejection, desertion, bitterness or betrayal. The past cannot be undone, but the wounds can be healed–wounds that gyrate around the deceptive self-image we project out to the world. We start living in lies, believing them to be the truths of our lives. We are scared to question our specious self-beliefs and confront them, pretending to be imperative, yet feeling undeserving, worthless, ugly, and despicable inside.

By setting foot in the realms of a primordial time when you got wounded in the first place and attempting to bring to light the darkest parts of our lives with courage and acceptance, these wounds can transform into immeasurable sources of strength.

Jesus once said, "And you will know the truth, and the truth will set you free."

Only once you truly acknowledge the wound, will you be able to gather the courage to forgive what keeps you from feeling complete and whole deep within. Once you move beyond the repercussions of these wounds, you'll understand their intent of relocating you to your true purpose. There is a relief, an absolution in knowing, in awareness and in understanding that this may not get healed immediately, but when it does, your chest will loosen up, releasing the heavy burden, and you will breathe completely freely again.

Emotional stress at any point of time affects us in life-altering ways. As adults when we are frazzled, the changes in body chemicals and hormones result in an inflammation of sorts causing cold, heart attack, etc. But when children or teens face such hardships, they are bequeathed with deep seated scars. These scars and wounds imperceptibly turn off the stress response. There is a great deal of research proceeding trauma and its correlation with childhood stress. Survey data reveals that people who did experience childhood trauma show symptoms of damaging-self and are triggered even by the smallest of stressors, overreact to everything and are less able to recover from the inevitable.

Science is now viewing human health and diseases in a new perspective altogether, studying the nexus between a difficult childhood and the diseases and illnesses experienced by an adult. The inflammatory chemicals in our body set the stage for diseases such as heart disease, cancer, fibromyalgia, chronic fatigue, fibroid tumours, irritable bowel syndrome, ulcers, migraines and asthma. Researchers are also exploring childhood wounds and their connection to chain smoking, overeating, over drinking and other varied behavioural patterns as a coping mechanism. Scientists from institutions like the Duke University in North Carolina, the University of California, San Francisco, and Brown University at Rhode Island point to the effects of childhood adversity on body cellular level, and how it prematurely age our cells and affects our span of life. Data also reveals that children who lost their parents, faced abuse, experienced neglect, or witnessed marital stress while growing up are more likely to develop cardiovascular diseases, lung diseases, diabetes, headaches, multiple sclerosis and lupus as adults. The chance of chronic fatigue syndrome is high in such individuals.

Remember, emotional pain cannot kill you but running away from it can. Deep inside our adult body sits an inner child waiting to be acknowledged and loved. In the process of protecting ourselves, we bury the wounded self alive, locking away our feelings. Childhood adversity hurts our mental and physical being, giving birth to psychiatric problems. A wounded child trapped within an adult bleeds and cries to be healed, to be free of living in these contradictory metaphors.

As you sow, so shall you reap, and the society reaps what it sows in nurturing its progenies. The wounded child wires its brain to cope with the newly discovered malicious world. Childhood abuse of any kind is not easy to get over, no matter how hard. But confronting evil and acknowledging its roots can help move a step closer to a more peaceful world that we all strive for. The evil may also have been a victim of this vicious circle of abuse. Our progenitors or early members of our lineage may not have dealt with their wounded child within, and passed on the provocations to continue the cycle. If we manage to heal the wounded soul within, peace shall reverberate, bringing a closure to the constant belief of inadequacy.

The wounded child needs you to forgive, which may not come easy at all, but it's your call at the end. Take your pick:

Persistent pain or final freedom?

The Teens & Me

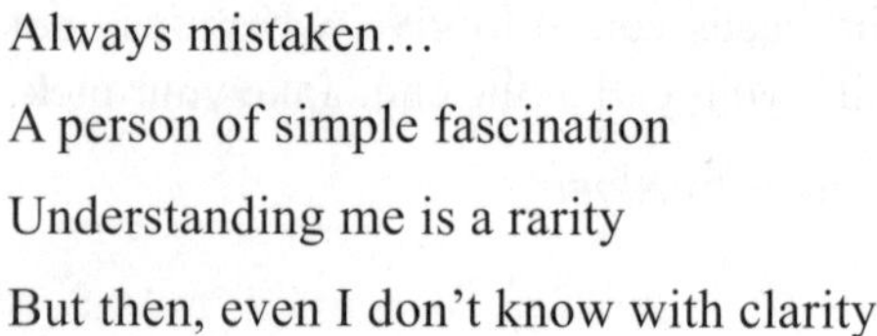

Always mistaken…
A person of simple fascination
Understanding me is a rarity
But then, even I don't know with clarity

Inside the mind lies light and dark
I am this spark
Igniting within, a flame
Here I come, proudly I proclaim
I am this glass
Fragile and easily broken
Waiting for the end, simply break and fall
Into the depths of helplessness, feeling small

Don't let me get stuck, I plead
While the divided me intercedes
Don't tell me I'm wrong to feel this way
My body, my mind, my friends, my world is changing everyday
Torn and scarred too many times

Showing my true colours would be a crime
Answering, “How are you?” with “I’m fine.”
Truth is seeking someone to read between the lines

This confusion beneath has consumed me for so long
But little did I know what exactly went wrong
For those years seemed to have a never ending note
Nothing lasts forever, every phase of life connotes
Life may have altered forever because of those years
For it brought me an understanding to now in here

I am a door
To pass through lessons always
Until the sun finally sets its blazing rays
And as this door witnesses goings and comings
Remember these would be the moments defining your being

-PaYal Jain

The Bumply Teen Ride

Do you remember the time when you felt sliced, divided and doled out by your own puzzled self? The time when you needed to prove your unique individuality, yet were busy finding ways to fit in? The time when you thought you knew everything, yet could not figure out a way to deal with your first heart break? The time when you experimented a ton of things (some you'll be embarrassed about all your life), the times of self-discovery? Yes, I am talking of the unsettled process of coming of age, which has left science bemused and parents muddled. It is the age of mood swings, the age of feeling totally misunderstood, the age of an emotional roller coaster with extreme highs and lows, the age when your peer group determines your cool quotient and so much more that creates a permanent sense of provocation, confusion and edginess. Isn't it strange that when almost all other species cope with this transition from infancy to adulthood with such relative ease, humans seem to struggle so much?

Scientists at the National Institute of Health (NIH) monitored the brain activity in young people, and found out that the human mind goes through considerable restructuring during the ages of 12 to 25 years rather than being fully developed by the end of childhood, as was once believed. The study at NIH also confirms critical physical changes between childhood and adulthood, resulting in impulsiveness, overwhelming mood swings, uncontrollable urge for risk-taking and all the unexplained actions that parents consider calculatedly intended to bring about misery and heartaches. These are in fact essential developments of the brain. Science is yet to solve the puzzle of adolescence, and like many others I too have not been able to hit upon a breakthrough in decoding the riddle of hormones. Gaining from my own experience and the experiences of others, however, I do tell to my teenage son that he is not alone, and knowing just that makes a huge difference. No matter how tough the play of your hormones makes your life, you should know that it isn't really the end of the world if things don't go the way you planned. Many people I know go on about how their teens were the best years of their lives–the thrill of experiencing everything for the first time, the first disco party, first time drinking alcohol, first love, first kiss, first night-out, first mess up you thought you could never get away with, but how all of us did. Many also talk about feeling like living under a microscope in those years, wherein everything had to be magnified and blown out of proportion, be it your feelings, your issues, your appearance, etc., like a theatrical performance featuring all the things that matter in the entire universe. I muse over some of my own experiences where I felt like I would never rise above the day of reckoning, the Armageddon, and how something would stay forever and continue pulling me down to the dumps.

Looking back, I wish I could travel time to meet my teen self and say a few things. I wish I could confront the superlative suffering years of my life; those painful times and tears that made me stronger and smarter, and sculpted me into becoming who I am today. I wish I could tell myself with a broad smile to not take life so seriously as this is the time where you're meant to mess up. When I look back, I see myself looking at two of me: one that the world saw–bold as brass, and the other one–scattered with fear, sadness, and confusion. I hark back to being both, how I would laugh out loud with my friends, being the coolest of the gang, and then cry for hours behind closed doors.

While my brain was still under construction, my mind was busy constructing the realities of life. Losing my mother at an early age added to the dramatic moments where my management of emotions felt like a test from hell. Shielding my fears with boldness, I felt confused and misunderstood. Hearing the whispers while walking through the hallways at school, or the chit-chat of relatives sitting in the drawing room made me identify my core that would carry me through all the losses, sadness, and even joys of the years ahead. If you think of it and look back upon your own life, it is the drama of the past that directs you to regulate your feelings and emotions in whatever way the world labels it–strong or weak.

My tearful moments of feeling misunderstood made me discover, learn and push my creative vision to its limits. In hindsight, I want to thank my teen self for introducing me to a passionate, zestful, hungry and creative future self. I still remember processing a photograph from the negative, having turned the garage to a dark room after investing hours in libraries during the non-google days, collecting information on how to do so. I would thank my teen self for making me realise the power of emotions, the power to make or break, and for allowing me to use the same push to go forward, to stop people from substantiating and verifying my worth, for making me see what I am capable of.

I realise that no period of my life comes close to being as difficult as those teenage years. Everything was forever changing, both physically and emotionally, and to top it all, I had to deal with the most intense situations back then, discovering heartbreak, anxiety, and peer pressure along the way. My teenage years remind me of the unpleasant time when I lost all stability in my life after my mother's death. Yet, there were periods of great adventure, living and working part-time, exploring my financial independence. If it weren't for those difficult times testing my limits, how would I have known what I believed in?

While my hormones and puberty were playing along mounting pus filled zits on my face, growing hair in strange places and making me bleed on a monthly basis, friendships were changing too which I misunderstood for cruelty back then. Over the years, I have learnt that no relationships are static. No matter how close, people will drift away after they've played their part in your life. As you get more confident in yourself, you realise that your group is not just to define your cool quotient. Some of those friendships remain forever, passing through the thick and thin, while some are only limited to their social media profiles. All these relationships taught me the value of a true friend and how to be one.

Teenage is the time when exploration marries new experiences. These experiences might be pleasant at times, or unpredictable and horrifying at others. You will find new dreams to follow, new persons to fall in love with, and a way to be comfortable with your body. You will overcome it all and everything will be okay. Eventually, the tide will turn and life will become even more different than what you had expected.

To my teen self,

Remember, sooner or later, you will recover and learn that this bumpy shift is just another defining moment of your being.

First Love

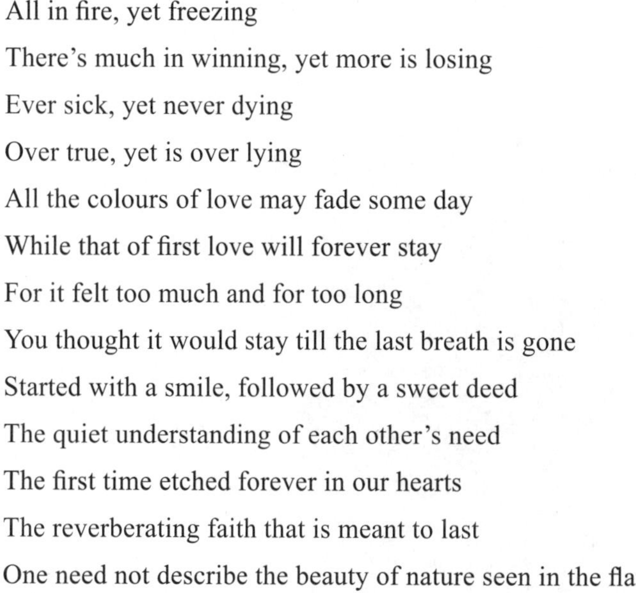

All in fire, yet freezing

There's much in winning, yet more is losing

Ever sick, yet never dying

Over true, yet is over lying

All the colours of love may fade some day

While that of first love will forever stay

For it felt too much and for too long

You thought it would stay till the last breath is gone

Started with a smile, followed by a sweet deed

The quiet understanding of each other's need

The first time etched forever in our hearts

The reverberating faith that is meant to last

One need not describe the beauty of nature seen in the flame red sunset

Whether you find true love in your first, or not in it yet

A beautiful relationship love is when you experience it in your heart

Like the spectrum of a rainbow sensed in the melody of a singing skylark

Just as the rhythm of rain needs no language, showing itself in a myriad ways

A loving heart, more than a thousand words, says

A beautiful relationship need not be defined

For love is not just smiles, looks or sleep of a broken bed

I went in search of love and lost myself

-PaYal Jain

Was It True Love?

Does your heart sink every time you think of your first love? Whenever you brood over counting on your heart to bequeath you with answers of what went wrong, or what it could have been, comes along inexplicable melancholy. The time may be long gone, but it still feels like yesterday. Years will pass, you may have moved on in many ways, but its memories will crawl back into your mind, fresh and vivid, making you realize that you never truly get over your first love.

You may fall in love again with an incredible person who completely sweeps you off your feet. Out of the blue, however, memories of your first love will pass through your mind and bewilder you in the most unexpected ways. They simply walk in, coming abruptly through the moments creating nostalgia, taking you back to the time when you first fell in love. There is something formidable about the experience of first love. It involves letting go of your heart's innocence and naivety, to take a willing dive into the unknown. The memories of all the 'firsts' in your life hold a special place in your heart, and this one a little more special and much stronger.

Your first friend, first pet, first cycle, first puff of the cigarette you stole from your dad's drawer, first loss teaching you a lesson regarding the people around you, first sip of beer, first kiss–all these *firsts* run deep in our blood, giving shape to our personality. There is something so stimulating and daunting about these first time experiences from our young times that as we grow older, we often recourse back to these points of no return in life. Memories of your first love are usually etched in your mind forever. The first stolen kiss while playing Spin-the-Bottle, feeling the sweet pants when you first hold hands with someone you call your boyfriend or girlfriend, when you suddenly become a believer of fairy tales and grow and irrepressible optimism despite the gloomy chances for your carefree state of mind that takes you to the great archives of documented love, and you want to be the next Romeo & Juliet, minus the tragedy.

There is no feeling of love like the first one for it was made special by its very novelty, thus lending a certain intensity to one's emotions. Ask anyone about their first relationship, their first cuddle, or the first time they explored the pleasures of physical intimacy, and their faces will light up with the memory of unforgettable experiences, giving them goose bumps. These memories take you back to the time when you felt this euphoria that transferred you to an entirely different world, making you discover your crazy madness inside. It doesn't matter when the cupid struck you, the first experience of romance and love will stay with you forever, be it good, bad, or muddled between the two. Our first love unfolds our idea and approach towards love for all our future relationships. The experience outlines the meaning of love for you, where you grade every single encounter romantic thereafter against your first.

If you experienced an unrequited or unreciprocated phase during the first time, where there was deep longing involved, then no love is love for you unless you feel this sort of a penetrating desire again. Experiences of love may come and go, and the memories of the first may fade, but the standard created by it remains until true love comes into the picture and changes the meaning for us.

First love is often confused with true love. First love is when a person enters your life, as if out of nowhere, and turns your world upside down. Each time you are in their radius, you feel thrilled and think that there is something special and even godly about them. You are swept off your feet and feel this relationship as so unique that nothing could compare to it in the entire universe. That's first love–magical and magnificent. Initially, it is innocent and ingenuous without any expectations or assumptions, neither is there an apprehension about where it will end up–together forever or painfully parted. Your first love takes the wraps off your insecurities, and you travel from jealousy to possessiveness to extreme dependence. The experience of first love is often confused and discordant, yet young lovers don't realize it and remain slaves to their feelings, confusing it to be true love. Then comes the 'falling apart' which does not hurt till you hit the bottom. When first loves come to an end, we long to hold onto them forever. First loves rarely last, yet the bitter sweet taste lasts long in your mind.

What you once thought would last forever may now seem very brief and transitory, or it could be true love — enduring, all-embracing, and plentiful. For sure, there is a chance that your first love is your only true love, but even when it is not, it does seem true while it lasts. Let us embrace the love that came along with our firsts, seconds or more, and raise a toast to love experienced truly, naturally and wholeheartedly.

Love is a strange feeling...

I don't know what it brings along, but when you smile wordlessly and still find it to be the best conversation, its charm is just out of the world.

मरीज़े इश्क़ जो जाओगे ,
जब बिन वजह मुस्का दोगे,
मिल कर जब साथ की, खुशी न समझ पायोगे,
इश्क़ ...इश्क़ से बढ़ कर है शायद
कैसे किसे समझाओगे ,
ऐसे ही नहीं मिला दीवानो का खिताब आशिक़ों को,
इश्क़ कर के देख, ऐ दोस्त,
खुशी खुशी, बशर्ते बावरे हो जायोगे |

– पायल जैन

Translation: You will know that you are in love for you will be smiling for no reason, unable to express the joy that comes with meeting the beloved. Love will be so much more that you won't be able to explain it for sure. No wonder, people in love are often called mad. Fall in love, my friend, and you will be crazily happy…this and more once you are a victim of love.

‘To Be’ And ‘To Being’

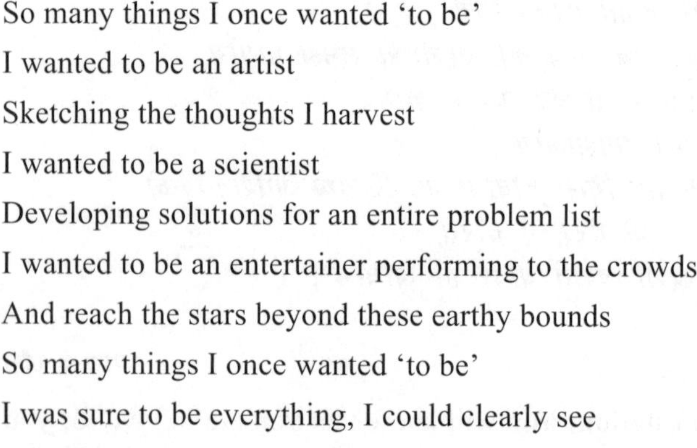

So many things I once wanted ‘to be’
I wanted to be an artist
Sketching the thoughts I harvest
I wanted to be a scientist
Developing solutions for an entire problem list
I wanted to be an entertainer performing to the crowds
And reach the stars beyond these earthy bounds
So many things I once wanted ‘to be’
I was sure to be everything, I could clearly see
And then my ‘to be’ was lost in rational necessity

So many things I once wanted ‘to be’
Happily exploring my passion, I was more than disposed
How I believed I could be anything my mind supposed
Voices from outside started whining in my head
They’ll help you build focus, everyone said
‘To be’ dreams were washed away by worries from years ahead
Fooled by societal success, I was misled
So many things I once wanted ‘to be’
I now hide in fear, in my heart of hearts
Imposed compulsions ripping me apart

So many things I once wanted 'to be'
There were dreams that did not let me sleep
Buried in the drill of making a hefty green heap
Friends and family meant good intentions
For pleasing others have brought worthy mentions
Handcuffed now in an painful pleasure
Bitten by snakes around the stated treasure
So many things I once wanted 'to be'
Being a puppet in the race was surely not on the list
The choices I take and the passions I resist

So many things I once wanted 'to be'
It all now seems like a mirage
I am tricked in my own suave panache
Would the once 'to be' ever come into being
What will others think — to such fears I cling
Justifying the choices I make
I am not that chosen one, for God's sake
So many things I once wanted 'to be'
In search of answers to 'what if'
Tired of the 'to be' and 'to' tiff

So many things I will always want 'to be'
Know for certain that in the end, I will always be me.

- PaYal Jain

I Wanted To Be...

The 'to be' has its home in our mind since the very early years of our life. One moment we want to be astronauts travelling to outer space, the next moment we want to be rock stars performing to a large crowd, or the prime minister of the country ready to change the face of its economy. Before we even know our inclinations and capabilities, the 'to be' is lost in the mysteries of necessity and demands of the world at large, gift wrapped in the words of our parents, peers, teachers and others. We do not explore the 'to be', limiting our potential to stay within the societal boundaries and align with its forces. The once 'to be' is handcuffed and the penalties imposed include following the rat race where your worth is measured against the number of zeros on your pay-check.

A quote by Gayle Forman has stayed with me for a long time now:

"Sometimes you make choices in life, and sometimes choices make you."

We are slaves to security — of a future and a comfortable life — at the cost of our unexplored 'to be'. It is not that we do not want to explore, but we wrap ourselves in the safety blanket and find it hard to balance time and energy to see the sight of this 'to be', to delve into our passion and follow our heart, so we bury ourselves in the sweet pain that gives us the pleasure of responsibilities being taken care of. Do you approve of the choices you have made in your life? How many times have you thought of not having pursued the degree you did in college? How many times have you considered telling your parents about your disinterest in training as a doctor and wish to pursue painting instead? How many times have you thought of quitting your job and taking a chance, but refrained from doing so because of numerous reasons? What choices are you made of?

As we grow up, we concede to the voices directing us the way our lives should be lived; the advice of our parents and teachers based on the society's definition of success sinks into our subconscious, making us have reservations about our once 'to be'. The notion of only one in a million actually getting what they want casts doubt on our own capability and begets feelings of inadequacy, and so we lose sight of our 'to be'. We stop believing in the possibility of being *the one*. Even when the belief manages to stay at times, the fear of unknown seeps down to our deepest insecurities, acceding to pick a path of safety and convention. And, we give up on our (once) dreams because we are scared, because our parents, advisors or peers don't get it, because we don't have support, because it is too risky, because we live under the compulsion to maintain a certain standard of living, because we are fooled by practicality and join the league of normality, running the race, being a crucible of our excuses, going about our lives.

As puppets, we become busy building a notable professional profile within a stipulated time, and fear going against the normal strain. Our once 'to be' start to appear as weird and irrational life choices. We once wanted to be everything (not literally letting our focus go haywire), wanted to try everything to find out who we really wanted 'to be', picking something from the n number of choices we had in our head and heart. Then, the outside voices started interfering with our dreams and barred us from experimenting. The so called secure routes still reminded us of the dreams that our 'to be' would have created.

It takes courage to defy the norm; it takes immense struggle and extraordinary attitude to bear the pressure of chasing your dreams — dreams that may give way to new ones over the years. The things that excite you show the way to your purpose. We dismiss these dreams, these explorations because we are worried about failure or prejudice, and in this hesitation, we prevent ourselves from immersing fully into the possible 'to be' options.

It is normal to have doubts about the choices you make. You don't have to pursue one if you don't want to. So what if you took up a wrong course in college, or was too busy pleasing your parents rather than following your passion. There is no point feeling resentful and hopeless now. You don't have to stick with it, nothing is forever. You can make a choice now and go down a different path, one of your choice. As humans, we are fascinated with the 'if'. If only I had stuck with my singing, if only I had taken up computer sciences, and the list goes on. You may feel like you've wasted a lot of time, but it is not too late. Most people are handcuffed to a postponement until they receive precise rewards, but then become addicted to these rewards that act as a speculation in our current quandary. The choice to either explore the 'what if' or not is always within your power. You may choose mediocrity and chase the golden mirage of success, but it'll make you feel incomplete and chained inside.

Imagine if Walt Disney had not explored his 'if'. He was turned down by many newspapers that told him that he lacked ideas. He was involved in animation ventures with others at that time, but then he gathered the courage to explore the ideas that excited him the most, and the rest is history. Harrison Ford, Mark Twain, Amitabh Bachchan, Steve Jobs, Ray Kroc and many others did explore their 'ifs' and chose not to be chained in the golden handcuffs. These golden handcuffs restrain us from trusting that buoyant, motivated, and passionate part of us that called the tune when we were younger.

Not all of us have one true calling, which is also fine. Don't go killing yourself to find that one 'to be'. It is also wonderfully whole to be a multipotentialite. Having many creative interests, exploring these pursuits and talents, bringing together this creative amalgamation and delving into the arenas of a myriad fields doesn't make you indecisive or non-committal. It simply defines you as exceptionally unique and innovative.

"Your time is limited; don't waste it living someone else's life. Don't be trapped by dogma, which is living the result of other people's thinking. Don't let the noise of other's opinions drown your own inner voice. And most importantly, have the courage to follow your heart and intuition, they somehow already know what you truly want to become. Everything else is secondary."

- Steve Jobs

The Caught Up Routine

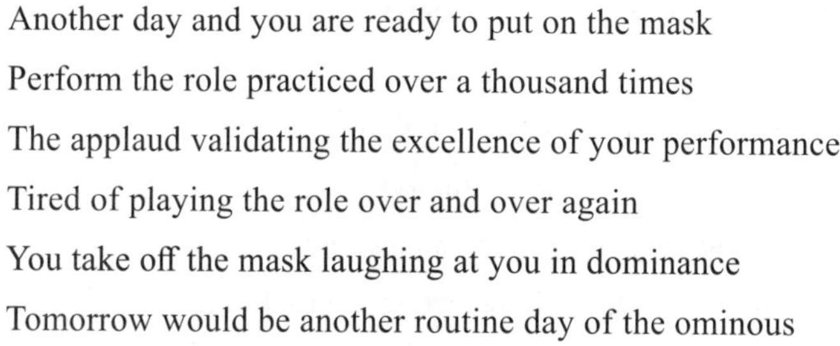

Another day and you are ready to put on the mask
Perform the role practiced over a thousand times
The applaud validating the excellence of your performance
Tired of playing the role over and over again
You take off the mask laughing at you in dominance
Tomorrow would be another routine day of the ominous

Knotted in ties of everyday tedium
Locked up with pangs of repetitiveness
Once again, you hinge on the countless amusing avenues
Easily thwarted, you seek more novelty
Soaking yourself in a plethora of amusements
Beaten down once again with tricky inducements

Drenching daily in showers of over simulation
Yet none to trust to come to rescue
Carrying on work or play in robotic modus
Catching up on the hot and happening
Pampering the self in compensation
Still missing on the fun destination

Once fun, they are just the things you do
And are now routines to follow
Performance props do not excite anymore
You immerse yourself in a busy routine
Fooled by hoaxed distractions
Whacked, confusing it for satisfaction

Bored or just experiencing boredom?
Look into your life and do answer
For each feeling comes with a meaning
Are you reasoning with the caught up routine?
Un-dealt boredom and clasping on emptiness
Choked with the routine, relying on nothingness

Choose not to lose track in everyday routine
Choose to admire life for real, not in the virtual world
Choose to do what you have always wanted to, once in a while
Choose to step out of the realm of your usual
Step out of reason, start small but do take your pick
Fun awaits on the other side of your call, while life ticks

-PaYal Jain

Bored Or Just Experiencing Boredom?

Do you feel at times as if you are locked in a life of routine, repetitiveness and boredom? Do the tedium and monotony add to the dullness, making you feel depressed? Do you find yourself easily bored stiff? It is quite strange to be bored in today's times when we have countless avenues of entertainment, including the world of the three 'w's, social media, multiplexes, shopping options, gaming, and almost everything which was once a stuff of dreams is now just around the corner, or a click of the technical magic away. With a plethora of amusement options at your fingertips, it is a paradoxical scenario where we still constantly find ourselves trapped in pangs of boredom.

With over stimulation and an over-load of information, our attention spans have gone down, which is why slow-paced activities like reading a book, researching for papers, sitting in long meetings and studying for longer hours tire and bore us easily, as we have grown so habituated to faster-paced incitements. As humans, we are ever excited to seek the novel, which produces a feel-good hormone — dopamine into our brains. As soon as the new gets old, however, the stimulus that thrilled us once no longer stirs up that liveliness, and eventually bores us. We then look for new sources of amusement, striving for that feel good high again.

In ancient times, the only thing humans engaged in was strategizing to survive, and that kept them away from boredom. Other times, they were either hunting for food and shelter, or protecting themselves from potential dangers which left them with no time for boredom.

However, there must have been times in your life when you felt too busy and bored simultaneously. Have you ever thought that being busy might just be a hoaxed distraction, which is why most of the human race insists on being busy to do away with boredom. Being busy successfully fools you by distraction, but definitely fails to incite fun.

We have countless entertainment choices around us, yet they fail in their purpose to engage us, and exalt the boredom rather than diminishing it, making us crave for alternate avenues. Nothing seems to please the brain for a long time, to quench the high or make us exciting enough to spend our valuable time on something. In today's times, we have so much at our disposal that we are forever pitter-pattering our fingers over the keyboard, our eyes glued to the screen, looking for distractions, watching Netflix, movies, updating ourselves on sports, technology, news and then communication with friends through our computer screens or smart phones via internet. Generally, people spend at least six to seven hours in front of screens every day. Even for varied activities engaging different neural systems, we choose to do the same on screens, like playing actual sports has been replaced by Xboxes. Everything we do is so overpowered and over stimulated with technology that 'fun' in life has become repetitively pedestrian. The result — we end up doing nothing substantial and thus get bored. This becomes a repetitive pattern, bringing nothing but ennui to our routine, making life monotonous.

Humans are social animals and having fun just in our own company is something we are not very comfortable with. Hence, we seek the company of others in almost everything in life. We have exercising partners, movie buddies, party groups and enjoy each other's company, often linking the same with not getting bored. Even then, you will find yourself experiencing dullness and lifelessness at times, despite the company.

If I asked you what you did yesterday or a day or two before, would your answer be 'the usual'? If you live the same routine every day, you lose track of what happens to you each day. There is nothing wrong in having a routine. Of course, it is a good thing that rescues you from the anxiety of dealing with uncertainty destabilizing your life. Most people grow up, find a job or a career, get married and have children, while completing the settle-down circle. Then there comes a time when they feel themselves as robots carrying on their tasks justified on the scales of responsibility, deadlines, significance and so on. They start to feel more and more insipid, uninterested and even depressed, yet they choose to continue functioning in that manner. Nothing seems to give them contentment, neither the weekend parties that go on till wee hours of the morning, nor the Sunday shopping for the latest designer collections at the most happening malls. Most of us don't recognise the boredom while getting caught up in the routine. Un-dealt boredom results in consequences like overeating, gambling, unsociable conduct, drug or substance abuse, impulsiveness, etc. It triggers apathy, laziness and even depression, affecting our relationships, outlook towards life, our thought process and eventually limiting our growth. Recognising the ennui early will help you break this monotony, and the sooner the better.

The first thing to recognise is whether you are bored or just experiencing boredom? The answer to this determined your happiness and satisfaction in life. Boredom is surely not 'a dearth of stimulus', for the more external stimuli we engage in, the quicker we get bored. Boredom is actually avoidance of self-rumination, inducing itself out of our inability to engage with something to our fullest potential. This monotony has become a social disease, damaging one's state of mind, affecting tolerance levels, diminishing focus and forcing one to indulge in compulsive behaviours like procrastination.

We depend on external spurs to slay our boredom, and define fun with our indulgence in company. We fear loneliness and aren't very comfortable paying attention to who we really are. But when we start doing so, it becomes an authentic mirror reflecting our thoughts that make us feel bored, instead of the external reality. We then recognize boredom as a state of mind resulting from a repetitive thought pattern. Embrace this boredom as an opportunity to present yourself with focus. Pay heed to what this monotony is hinting at. Take a look at your to-do list, and indulge in activities that stir up creativity. It is not the responsibility of your friends or family to bring you out of this boredom, so do not dwell in self-pity. Break the monotony and get involved in something different every day. Start small, for you may get apprehensive about the workings of whatever new thing you pick up. Resolve the problem before it is too late, for it is the time to fight back.

Soul In The Cage

Our souls locked in a restriction cage,
Caged, we spell a manipulative rage…
Was splashed in a puddle once,
Amid little joys and delighted with just the buns…
From toddlers to controlled beings for gains,
Situations, responsibilities or calculated attains…
Frolicking in the freedom within,
Feeling like a stranger in my own skin...
Seeking what affluence could yield,
Acting things that appealed…
Judgement over clothed-mind ways,
Caging my soul in a myriad ways…
It is sad that we can't breathe or feel the freedom,
Of our own thoughts and actions, as if infused with venom…
In the trance of a mundane thought, I lay
Tenor of my entrapment in an eccentric way...

As I glowered, looking out to the world,

Everyone caged, unaware, unheard.

- PaYal Jain

In The Cage

Living in constant conflict, our flesh and soul present a dichotomy that most of us reflect on in our lives, representing a world of out-and-out upheaval. The pretence of the mask worn, musing over a set of circumstances, tears your soul apart while bringing about unrest, confusion, disharmony and frustration in incarcerating and chaining one in a cage of convenience.

How many times have you felt not truly alive anymore, but simply existing, doing chores, passing time, waiting for this or that to end when your physical body gives up, winding down the inner turmoil, putting an end to the formality of merely living.

I once read a quote, "In order to live your life to the fullest, you must think about your death every day."

At that time, I was in college and was too busy planning my life ahead to think about my death at all, but it did hit me hard later in life. Steering through the ups and downs of life, I did explore various domains, excelled in different lines of work, mounting a professional life. From running a family business to being able to achieve feats of success in event management, from designing curriculum and running a play-way school to superintending a corporate house squad, inadvertently being introduced to journalism and then being a role model to many, I have held many career options over the years, all of which I am very proud of. The continuous shifts in my career interests came with pinnacles of success, but not without occasional bouts of emptiness and vagueness, as if something was not my life's purpose or calling.

With a loving family by my side, a lucrative and challenging flashy career and a roaring social verve, my life was written off as a "fulfilled" one. Yet, this fulfilled life perturbed me often, making me unhappy and realise the void within. I divulged these feelings to my family, friends, and workmates, and a majority of then stated something along the lines of, "That's life." In my quest for truth and seeking the missing part of this jigsaw puzzle, I dived deep into my own self and thought hard about the same. I did receive my answers and was reminded of the quote, "In order to live your life to the fullest, you must think about your death every day."

A life labelled as 'fulfilled' may quench and satiate animate (food, sex, family) and social (wealth, power/fame, knowledge) desires, but can never ever compensate for feeling truly complete and in unanimity with your soul. Most of us feel discordant and dead inside as our soul has wearied itself in the process of perpetual burial of the self to build a 'fulfilled' life. When I was flicking through the vacuity inside me, I reminded myself of my breathing which was a testimony of me being NOT-dead inside. There surely was a force that kept my breath going, which was to recognize what I was looking for.

कोई तो है मुझमें मुझको संभाले...

के बेकरार हो कर भी बरकरार हूँ...

- पायल जैन

Translation:

Someone in me is holding on to me…

Persistently uneasy, yet resilient…yet I am…

A lot of answers came to me, asking these simple questions:

If I were to die today, what ideas, what dreams, what abilities, what talents, what gifts would die with me? And then the discovery happened, thus releasing me from the cage…

It takes courage to see within and seek answers. To live a fulfilled life, sometimes you have to risk everything for a dream that no one can see but you. Death can come knocking any moment without a warning, but would we have lived for our dreams till then, would we have used our time here without conflicting the within? If yes, we would have lived a fulfilled life.

When we are young and full of life, most of us aspire to learn new things, are infused with enthusiasm and charged with ideas, always rummaging around for opportunities to make a difference in this world and leave our mark. Most of us have hopes, goals, dreams, happiness, and millions of other emotions, and we live them without pretence, being the person who we really are. When we are young, most of us want to make our own mistakes and take our own decisions. We enjoy the process but then grow cautious, wedged between the mundane. When others love and respect us for the same, we keep on performing the pretence, often falling in love with it too, growing attached to these masks. We simply go on feeding this identity despite feeling lost and disconnected, and die much before we actually do.

Heard the phrase, *died at 25, buried at 75*?

Look within.

This phrase gives a clue for you to look within, pull yourself up and free yourself of the zombie mode. Look around and find your motivation to come to light.

"So may the outward shows be least themselves:

The world is still deceived with ornament.

In law, what plea so tainted and corrupt,
But, being seasoned with a gracious voice,
Obscures the show of evil? In religion,
What damned error, but some sober brow
Will bless it and approve it with a text,
Hiding the grossness with fair ornament?
There is no vice so simple but assumes
Some mark of virtue on his outward parts."

— William Shakespeare, The Merchant of Venice

Monday Blues

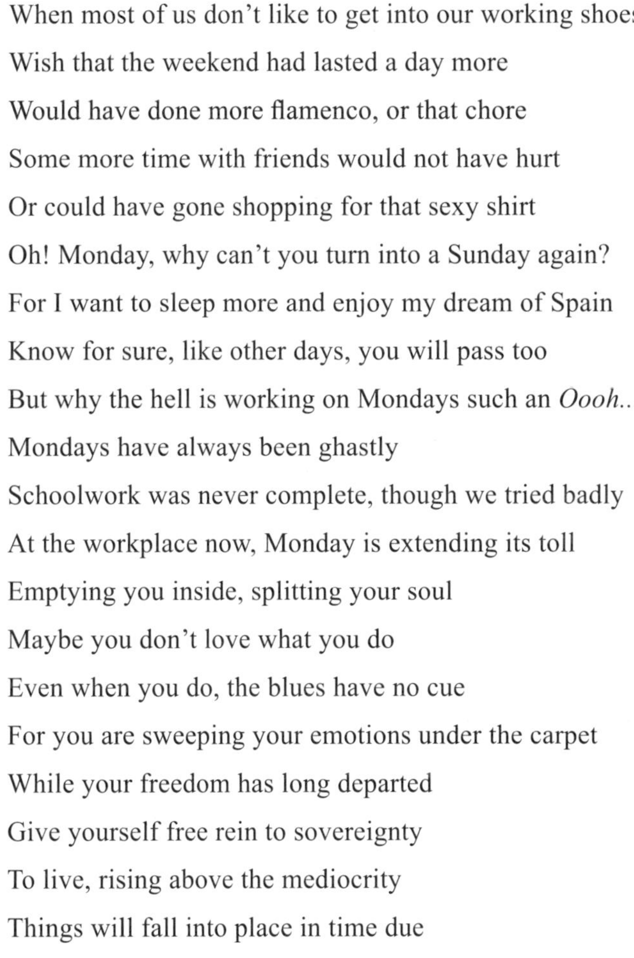

When most of us don't like to get into our working shoes
Wish that the weekend had lasted a day more
Would have done more flamenco, or that chore
Some more time with friends would not have hurt
Or could have gone shopping for that sexy shirt
Oh! Monday, why can't you turn into a Sunday again?
For I want to sleep more and enjoy my dream of Spain
Know for sure, like other days, you will pass too
But why the hell is working on Mondays such an *Oooh...*
Mondays have always been ghastly
Schoolwork was never complete, though we tried badly
At the workplace now, Monday is extending its toll
Emptying you inside, splitting your soul
Maybe you don't love what you do
Even when you do, the blues have no cue
For you are sweeping your emotions under the carpet
While your freedom has long departed
Give yourself free rein to sovereignty
To live, rising above the mediocrity
Things will fall into place in time due

Once you know what's tossing inside of you
Countenance your core
Delightful and fulfilled, you will feel for sure
For life will hold a purpose and a meaning
A Monday or not all days will you be gleaming
Soon, blues will go away with the hues
As you get ready in your working shoes

- PaYal Jain

Putting On The Working Shoes

The demanding, challenging, gruelling and hectic nerve-racking day that comes every week following the weekend brings along a ton of work while reminding us that we aren't so cool and carefree after all. A large number of people complain about 'Monday Blues'. Are you one of them too who gets infected with this distressing flux of despair, anxiety or stress every Monday morning? Is dressing up to take on the responsibilities of the day or week something you look to escape every Monday? If that is the case, chances are that you are among the many who may perhaps be victims of Monday Blues.

'Blues' refers to sadness. The colour blue has always been used with a negative connotation in english texts. Your hands turn blue with cold, or you are 'blue in the face' when exhausted from anger or strain. The association comes from the colour representing a lack of blood in the human body, thus indicating low energy, strength or willingness. Over the weekend, you might have indulged in weekend gluts, partied more, shopped more, took that hiking trip, and did what you did in a carefree manner. Letting go of this freedom after the weekend creates a dip in your energy level. Thus, Monday manages to take its blue toll on many people, yet some manage to pull it off pretty well.

Studies reveal an alteration in the rise of cortisol levels with work-related stress during work days, and a drop in the same over weekends. It was also found that individuals are more satisfied and happy during the weekends, while weekdays incite the contrary responses, without any major disparity between Mondays or other work days, barring the second half of the last working weekday, when your spirits are high and mood is lifted unaided. Mondays bring in the extra stress and seem dreadful for they represent a full week of work ahead and compromise your freedom hitherto being enjoyed. Monday Blues can happen to anyone, be it a professional or a student, for he may be stressing over the submission of an unfinished project. Monday blues do not necessarily imply that you hate your job; some may love their professional opus and yet be inflicted with it. It does not necessarily mean that one is sad, it could simply hint at the challenges at hand.

Typically, we schedule things to the last moment which underpins the blues. Spend a little extra working time on Fridays to take care of killing chores. Students too will feel more positive each Monday morning if their Sunday night is free of last-minute project panic. Monday Blues are nothing but a desired extension we crave for. You may feel a bit of desolation when you put on your working shoes and get on for the first time every week, but these blues are just a reflection of your lack of interest, or feeling down. So, the next time you say it is just Monday Blues inspiring lethargy in you, it is time to introspect if you are casting a shadow over your infuriation towards life? Figure out what your attitude is towards it all.

As humans, we are at our fullest potential when we are allowed to be free. When we start a career, we can't wait to be at the top, but then we realise that we have to give in our freedom in numerous modus operandi to fit in and do a lot of things that do not resonate with our checkboxes. We then blindly follow the band wagon, dragging ourselves the entire week with proverbial carrots dangling in front of us — living authentically free only on the weekends. We forget that we shouldn't have to wait for the weekend to have fun or be happy. We have to decide on creating these moments of freedom every day. We have to decide for giving up something transitory to have what we ache for in the long term.

Monday blues are an illusion our mind tricks us to believe. Your inner self-belief cons you with situations and conditions, turning your Monday blue. The blues, while you are wearing your working shoes, make you feel frazzled and stressed is a way of giving an inkling of not letting emotions and feelings sweep under the carpet. Ruminate over what it is that you are dreading or is causing you grief. You may be in love with your job, but hate your boss. Think of the changes in the external or internal panoramas you entail, abstaining from feeling this way. The possibilities are endless. Through conversations alone with the self and others, clarity can be achieved, else we may be misled by figments of our imagination. So if you hate your boss putting pressure on you, it is time to comprehend the thoughts and feelings that this pressure is manoeuvring inside you.

'Monday blues' is just another hoax playing a downer on you. We are programmed and conditioned for years to feel in a certain manner. Birthdays are supposed to make us feel good, a vacation is supposed to elate our mood. We make these anticipated predictions time and again, including the one for Mondays. We become so focused over these predictions and what we are supposed to feel, that we take no notice of how we actually feel. That is one of the prime reasons why the third Monday of January is supposed to be the gloomiest day of the year, despite there being no scientific evidence to support it. Thinking it as the most depressing day of the year, we start paying more attention to the negative events around it. Science is now recognising the fact that when we hold some expectations regarding an event, our actions start falling in line with our expectations.

If your self-prophecy has worked in the past and has successfully programmed you to hate Mondays, maybe it is time to make it work in your favour and change your perspective. Imagine how Mondays are not fully lived, due to the dread over Monday Blues. Take chances, embrace the uncertainty and accept your failures to move on. Simply by changing your perspective, you will give a free rein to change your life. Days of the week won't even matter then. It will be a beautiful morning every day and you will be thankful to be alive, looking forward to the times ahead, working on realms that contribute to your fulfilment and purpose, and be at peace with your core.

The Put Off Puzzle

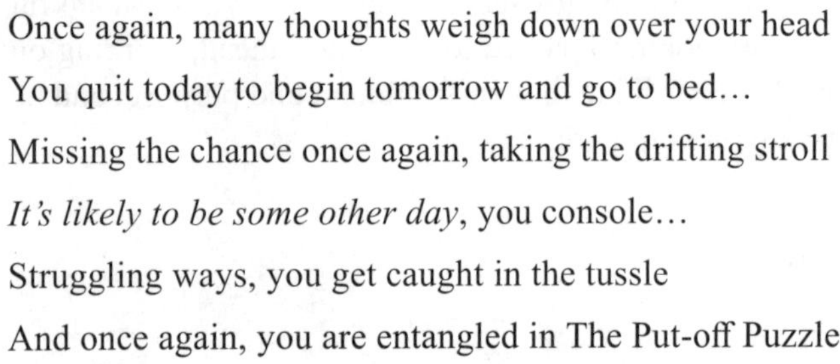

Once again, many thoughts weigh down over your head
You quit today to begin tomorrow and go to bed…
Missing the chance once again, taking the drifting stroll
It's likely to be some other day, you console…
Struggling ways, you get caught in the tussle
And once again, you are entangled in The Put-off Puzzle

Crushed between the to-do and will-do duality
Overwhelmed, coming back to the actuality…
Goals seem far away and dreams hazy
For you are standing in your way, being lazy…
Leaving behind for another day, you juggle
Beaten one more time by The Put-off Puzzle

The Put-off is always there,
Controlling your thoughts with a daunting stare...
For you succumbed to its tricks
Filled with hopes, yet neglected with inflicts…
Playing with your mind again, making you hustle
The mighty Put-off Puzzle.

Things will get finished today or tomorrow at the most,

Conformity is again haunted by the put-off ghost…

The paradox of put-off makes you doubt your ability now,

For things you were once determined to do are hoaxed with how…

The Put-off wears that maliciously evil smile,

Glancing at the To-do pile…

Are the dreams, the goals, all its worth?

May be it's time for a new attitude's birth…

For putting off the put-off may help at the start,

And going for what you wish in your heart.

- PaYal Jain

Kajoi

Counting On Tomorrow

You have once again successfully managed to escape from what needs to be done and given in to what you are doing. Procrastination has once again played a tactful devil that took over the throne and muddled your mind, paralyzing you from moving forward.

And so you escape onto social media, marking favourite tweets, having mood swings over who said what, accusing the delinquents while feeling sorry for the victims, throwing yourself over to an overload of information while feeling sorry for n number of things in the world. You escape on to playing video games, or just doing not-so-important things that take you nowhere you long to be.

How many times have you committed yourself to doing something, then ended up not doing it? You may have your own reasons. I always had mine. One usual suspect is 'the time was not right'. This is no more than a hollow defence, a lame excuse we use to justify not seeking our goals and dreams. What is the guarantee that when your 'right time' arrives, you will still be alive? We dress the procrastination, the put-off puzzle, in the attire of circumstances, blaming the specific situation we feel we are stuck in.

"You may delay it, but time will not."

You may delay and put-off your to-do list, but time will continue to tick onwards making you give up control in front of the naked sword of Procrastination.

There are two forces that put people either into action or inaction. It depends on which of the two is sturdier — pain or pleasure. Are you tortured by the thought of leaving your cosy and warm bed on chilling winter mornings so you can hit the gym for a workout session? Some will say it's totally worth the pain, while some will pass. When the pleasure to remain sleeping in their warm beds is stronger than their pain of having an unfit body, they will choose to sleep. Some people derive pleasure from smoking, and the reasons behind this pleasure vary from smoker to smoker. The emotion of pleasure they associate smoking with is stronger than their urge to quit. Despite knowing it is injurious to health, they will continue to smoke till the time pain keeps winning over pleasure. For instance, if they are told that by smoking, they will lose their life to a long breeding cancer, they might stop, for the pain that they associate with death will now dominate their pleasure of smoking.

Our priorities revolve around pain and pleasure, and to no one's surprise, we are more likely to delay the things we don't attain any pleasure from. One often falls into the 'I will do it later' trap and tends to pay meagre attention to distant deadlines and avoid them till the last minute for their unpleasant nature. The puzzling put-off attitude towards the things that matter, things that one is capable of, serves as enough reason behind our procrastination, as the prospect of failure appears painful to us. At a subconscious level, one feels insufficient when one has to be in action, and the fear of failing frames the action of inaction. It is this fear that concocts excuses like — 'I didn't have enough time' or 'this is not the right time', 'I will do it once things are more favourable' and so on.

Thus, we get stuck in the paradox of putting-off our goals and dreams, as well as the pleasure of having what feels right. On one side, we want to get there and dream about it day and night, putting our trust in our inner potential, while on the other side, we fear 'what if we don't get there' and get trapped in the cycle of postponing it forever. The fear of failure overpowers the excitement around success. When we don't take a step towards the image of success that we have constructed in our head, we reinforce the fear and then the ego steps in with its excuses.

Some people may even foster the put-off stance for the pleasure in living on the edge. The excitement of almost failing stimulates their performance and propels them to do the task better. Some may procrastinate due to the fear of greater responsibilities that may come with the success. While the put-off puzzle turns more bewildering, the outcome becomes an endless cycle of anxiety, evasion, and disappointment. Nothing productive is achieved, making us anxious all the time with guilt hanging over our head. One can never really relax and enjoy then, because the mind is constantly occupied with what one should be doing.

Have you ever wondered why successful people take action despite all the obstacles, while most other people are not willing to work for what they want even when they have all the opportunity to do so? They know that they need to do something, but still don't do it. Behind this disorganized, lazy, or even careless feeling sits a capable individual who just can't seem to figure a way out of this put-off maze.

If you are willing to solve the puzzle and introspect, ask yourself if you are more worried about things going wrong and the reaction of others over your failure over even trying. You abscond from realizing your limits when you put things off and justify not trying things because they make you anxious.

When you consistently give yourself excuses for not doing something, you eventually start believing them. Be careful of what you tell yourself. You surely are better than your excuses, which are anyway stopping you from achieving your goals. Break the task, delegate the work, ask for help and do all that is required. Let not your excuses stop you from getting where you want to be. The root problem is that we all want to do great things and we want to do them fast, but remember that every big thing started small once. Focus on taking one step at a time and begin with that. To put off the put-off attitude, let that step be so tiny that it feels effortless. If you want to run a marathon, start running one block first, then gradually push your limit, continuing the drive to the second, and so on.

सोचने से कहाँ मिलते है ,
ख्वाबों के शहर...
चलने की ज़िद भी ज़रूरी है,
मंज़िलो के लिए |

Translation:

You don't reach the city of dreams by only the power of your imagination.

Your dreams, goals, and true desires will only be accomplished with your stubbornness to walk in that direction.

In today's world, when distractions are many, it is common to procrastinate. But if we are always submitting to these distractions, we put ourselves in the vicious circle of lack of productivity. At some point of time in our lives, we limit ourselves from the pleasure of seeking who we want to be. Remember who you want to be, write it and keep your reasons strong in your head. Remind yourself of the feeling that you'll get when you become what you want to be. It may not be easy to escape the putting-off, but it'll be worth having a fulfilling life that you strive for.

"Seek not who you are, seek who you want to be and never let the charismas of the put-off puzzle allure you, or fall to the obstacles of excuses, for you are what you own."

Failure

Failure...
Ever wondered why it is so important?
This is what it takes to succeed,
This is what it takes to lead,
Only if you have been on that back seat.
Failure...
For it's not the end of the world,
It's just the times; things did not work,
For that's what makes you strive through,
To have you gain and let the pain shoo.
Failure...
Failure, my friend, is an opportunity
For you to not give up on your dream,
And keep going and do, impossible as it may seem,
This time now that you think you have failed...
Get up and try one more time with the experience just gained.

- PaYal Jain

Winner Is Just A Loser

Have you ever seen a coin with just one side? It is very difficult to even imagine one, for it gives an impression of an incomplete picture. We all have heard a thousand times that every coin has two sides — substantially different from each other, like chalk and cheese, but it is only when these dramatically diverse sides are together that they make a real coin with a truly lasting value. If you have never lost, you won't know how it feels to win; if you have never been sad, you won't know what joy is. It's thus very important to be able to understand both sides of life's metaphorical coin.

What does it means to you when someone calls you a failure? Of course, none of us like it. We don't come equipped to handle it. While exploring thc atrociousness around failure, I realised that it is not the failure that we fear, but the criticism and embarrassment that follows which devises the struggle. Baffled by our own lack of ability to handle failure, we bury ourselves under layers of embarrassment, feeling that we are not good enough, or feeling like a loser in life, but all this makes success even harder to achieve. It is when you peal away all the layers of shame that your failure turns into a phenomenal thing.

Flip through the pages of history and you will come across thousands of celebrated failures. In fact, the most successful people in the world are the ones who have endured the most failures in life, repeatedly failing time and again. However, there is something else that they did repeatedly — they kept following their path and never called it quits. They made the choice to overlook all obstacles brought to them by failure in the process and refused to be blinded by the threat of ignominy. Despite being knocked down many times, they continued on their passage. They won because they tried one more time after each loss, and once more till they achieved the glory of success.

"A winner is just a loser who tried one more time."– George M. Moore Jr.

You cannot escape failing. Right from your birth till now, you must have suffered through a torrent of failures and you did survive them. Not just that, you learned from these failures and improved your life by them. Of the two, success and failure, a failure will always teach you more, allowing you to achieve new insights on life.

Failing is also a path of self-discovery, putting your attitude, your strength, your focus, your determination, your hunger to succeed and everything else to test. All of this combined should be greater than your fear of failing in the attempt. So try, fail, try again and fail again if that is what it takes, but fail better (Samuel Beckett) than the last time and then rise up from these failures, get a hold of your mistakes and try one more time.

"Failure is just the beginning of success."

Sometimes, success is misunderstood as achieving the goals set by the 'why's and 'wherefore's of the outside world. That is the reason why at times it does not feel right even after being a smash hit. Assess and evaluate what you want to achieve while remaining the person you aspire to be. Only then will you witness being infused with an atypical vigour where you are not afraid of failing, not afraid of trying. Whenever there is a hurricane in your life and the waves are devastating, stay still and calm, and say it out loud that you are ready. Even if you fall, you can rise again. Remember, there is nothing that can come between you and trying again. It's never too late to take another shot. Colonel Harland Sanders, the founder of KFC, set out at the age of 65 with nothing but a $105 social security check and a recipe of what is now the most popular fried chicken brand in the world.

Biographies of many successful people in the world — J.K. Rowling, Steve Jobs, Richard Branson, Oprah Winfrey, Albert Einstein, Walt Disney, and so on — all failed many times in their life before they conquered their respective fields. Failures did not stop them as they turned them into lessons and bounced back. Stories of their success prove that in order to succeed you need to develop the power of resilience to overcome disillusionment, rejection, as well as dejection.

Whether you are an entrepreneur striving to earn a name for yourself in the business world, or someone who leaves everything behind in the search of a worthwhile unknown, you will have to face rejection, failure and denunciation at some point or another. It will compel you to procrastinate or give up on your goals, but it is when we allow these heavy-duty emotions to sail our life's ship that we allow it to smash against a rocky obstacle and break down.

I have failed many times and in many things in my life. All these experiences evoked much emotional turmoil within me, and side-tracked me from the lessons I should have learned. I threw myself into the agony of rout, while missing out on the thrill of success. As a consequence, it affected my behaviour in the most unproductive way. All this while, I've never forgotten the feeling of being stuck when things just didn't work out the way I expected them to be. Then, I realised that I could not let my ship hit rock bottom.

In facing the fear of rejection and the criticism that follows, interpreting the same and staying focussed on achieving your goals, you will need to ride with resilience.

Failure is a reassurance that you tried, no matter the result. It may rip you apart and tear you down, but it can also build you up in ways you never thought were plausible, adding to your knowledge. The saddest sentence I have come across when people speak about their lives is, "It might have been…" It reflects a strange melancholy enveloping regret. You will never know what is on the other side till you walk the distance in that direction.

"Regrets don't provide opportunities, failures do."

No one likes failure, but if I tell you that you will definitely succeed after going through a churn of countless failures, would you still risk it? Most of us will not find the courage to risk it and take the turbulence head-on. We would rather lock our dreams up in a deception of contentment. Observe a child trying to walk for the first time. He or she falls many times, but is not afraid to risk it again and fall again, till his or her chest swells with pride with the first few steps taken in continuity. The story of failures only starts here. We fail in school exams and are accorded with punishments. We don't meet a deadline at work, and fear demotion. A heartbreak is often good enough to make us fear love for a long time after. It is a sad truth that the world does not teach you that there is no winning without losing, but life does…only if you are willing to learn.

Silly Things And Big Egos

One more relationship glooms
One more relationship, down it goes...
Silly things and not calling them so...
Are we still on the same page?
Or am I taking the wondering boat's row...
Your smile makes my day
Looking at you makes my heart melt...
Thousands of things, we didn't say but surely felt...
For they will make you look silly...
How can you sound so frilly...?
Sometimes *are you fine?* or *I am okay* has more...
Let go the silly things and the big egos
For two and two are not always four...
Is it a yes or a no?
Ask and let go...
Won't harm or hurt as it may sound...
Just lose that pretence and hold your ground...
Well now, that's the difficult part
Echoes I hear...
What if I am looked at as super weird...?

Again, the thought bangs back
Why to take it out from the self-rack...
The reasons will always be the same...
So, are you game?
Challenge and let it echo...
Silly things and big egos

- PaYal Jain

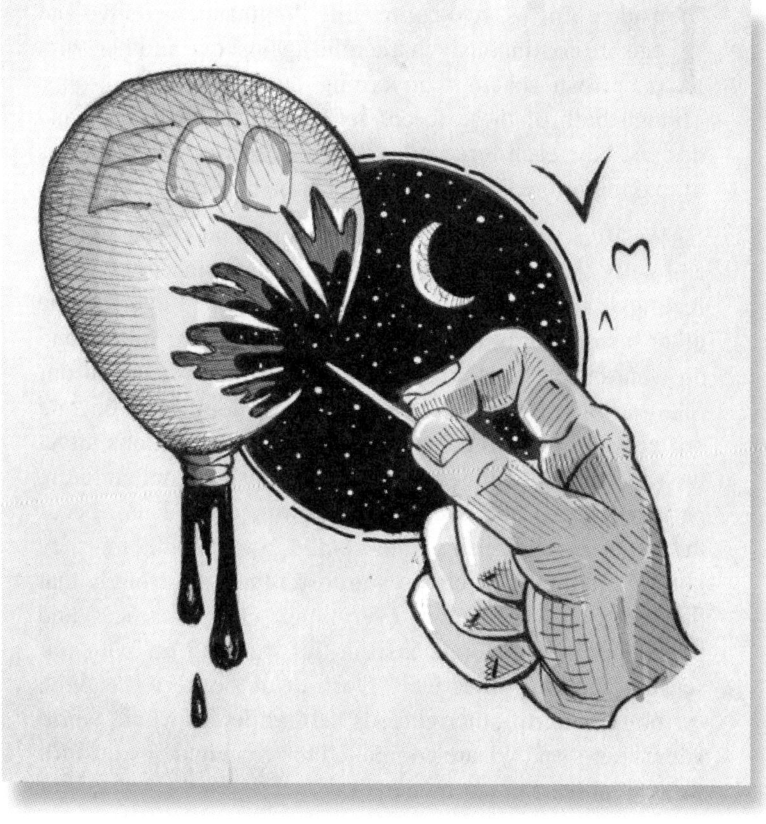
EGO

The Ego Effect

Inside all of us, two contrasting dominances — love and ego are continuously in a scuffle against one another, with their own schemes governing our life's relationships. Though both of these forces reflect our needs, wants, and desires, how each force rules the roost serves as the genesis of making or breaking any relationship.

We all have an ego, and when it comes into play, all silly and petty things cause colossal chaos, bringing in negative feelings and causing unhappy relationships. Love, on the other hand, simply takes ego out of play. If we follow and do what our heart is directing at, love would rule in all our relationships. Most times, however, we don't look beyond our ego and our assumptions, and these assumptions affect the way we go about being in relationships with our children, partner, friends and everyone else around us. There occur things in a relationship one should brush aside for they don't matter, but one chooses to foster them so strongly that they start to overshadow everything. Our inferences and presumptions proliferate insecurities, running off with our sense of thinking objectively. Our side of the story is enough for us to confirm our righteous self while the whole world goes wrong, and we are compelled to prove it at any cost till we win, at least in our own eyes.

Every big fight starts with a silly delusion. Recalling one of mine with my spouse, it began innocently enough as we were to leave for a vacation after a long period of following our hectic schedules. I had already begun to imagine us sipping cocktails at a bar or rejuvenating ourselves with a refreshing swim in the sea. As I was packing for the much awaited beach vacation, I expected my spouse to take part in the excitement, help me pack, and explore things to do at the planned destination. He did none of it, but was spaced out on his device, glued to football matches. I got upset and let out my angst, but he turned defensive. One thing led to another and it grew into an ugly fight, eventually leading to the trip being cancelled. Our egos did not allow us to ask for help, or to feel sorry for not being demonstrative about our emotions as we were so involved in proving our own subjective realities. Now when I think of it, it was sheer stupidity on our part to cancel the much awaited trip over a silly fight. Secretly though, I kept waiting for my spouse to come and wheedle me, but all was in vain.

Over the years, I have realised that this ego makes us miss out on amazing people in our lives. Instead of living our true selves in a relationship, we let the past experiences take over and let our egos operate all our relationships. In justification to protect the self, the ego resorts to winning even at the cost of disrespect, intolerance, blame, putting-down, distrust, frustration, resentment and self-doubt. Neither in the relationship recognizes that this victory is actually putting the relationship at a loss.

When in a relationship, we constantly evaluate it at a subconscious level, in terms of security, acceptance, importance, etc. whether we identify the same at a conscious level or not. Some answers do not have a validating explanation to the current situation, but when you start to remove the layers off years of unresolved conflicts triggering the reaction, you start to understand the other's perspective, putting your ego aside.

Ego can ruin close bonds, turn friends into foes, family members distant. Smilingly, it puts a wedge in all your relationships in some way or the other. If you have had a string of unsuccessful relationships with friends and family, maybe it is time to introspect and consider your own ego. Perhaps you got hold of the wrong end of the stick, and were draping it with self-esteem all this while.

A person's ego is driven by internal insecurities and is affected by what others say or the external factors, while people with a high self-esteem are only affected by internal factors such as their self-belief or personal vision. People with big egos are always in the process of covering up those insecurities by placing themselves centre stage, pretending to be most important. Conversely, those with a high self-esteem are comfortable with who they are and accept themselves with all their flaws. When we accept our flaws, hearing about them from others doesn't hurt. The conflicts, the unresolved issues, always hinder our ability to establish new relationships. Understand your true self and accept the fact that you cannot be right all the times. Being in accord with your weak areas will not be easy initially, but being able to own up to your faults will confer a sense of freedom on you.

Nothing will ruin you more swiftly than your ego, for the best or worst side of a relationship. Sometimes, you may be stuck in an unworthy relationship because your ego doesn't want to accept that you were wrong for getting into one in the first place. We thus hang on to a relationship even when it does not feed our ego in any way. This applies not only to the projected 'bold, intelligent and outspoken' clan, but also to the evidently righteous and empathetic people. Our ego doesn't allow us to see our own limitations and presents an illusion in most of our relationships. You can't expect perfection, because you are not perfect yourself. Look inside and courageously assess yourself within. The camouflage will then disappear and your words, thoughts and actions will fall in alignment with your relationships.

We all are slaves of our egos and we cannot get rid of it entirely, but we can choose to either feed it or starve it. Experiencing true love means abandoning our ego's assertions and assumptions, and there is always fear when we make that decision. Relations, bonds and connections are meant to be the most beautiful aspects of a human's life, but they are sadly the most complicated ones too, courtesy the 'ego'. All humans, at their core, want to love and be loved, yet when we find true love, we withdraw, put up walls, and sometimes even run away, fearing getting hurt. We put our relationships under the scrutiny of our ego's assumptions convinced of our judgements. You can still choose to be free from doubt and return to the light of love.

Relationships require concern, compassion and equivalence. "People are lonely because they build walls instead of bridges," said Joseph F. Newton very rightly.

These walls of ego and defence, the longing to always be right will keep wrecking relationships between co-workers, siblings, relatives and partners. At some point, you will need to smash the wall and let go of your ego and those fears, for there is no greater risk than loving with all your heart, and no risk more worth the shot to get there.

Love Or Convenience In Love

Love, a need or a convenience?
Incite the relationship riddle,
And suddenly, you are caught in the middle…
Pulling the wool over everyone's eyes
Weeping within while conning them with smiles
Abandoning love time and again
For reasons bequeathing a pleasing pain…
Caught in the dichotomy of feelings and needs,
The heart resists, disapproves, yet concedes…
Things of future the heart may fear
Can all be resolved when love is here…
For all you have to do is entrust
And rise above the greed, filth and lust
Terrified, you shut the heart's door in dismay
Tricking your mind in every possible way…
Love awaits while true happiness calls
Scared stiff, you conveniently evade the fall,
The fall that could make you invincible, as if you could fly

Soaring with bliss, emotions so high…

The fall you purposely thwart

For doubts surrounded with shouts society has taught

Once again, confined from experiencing love in its truest form

Pretending love than exploring seems to be the norm

For you have been trapped for long in love's prejudice

Drawing a veil of perfection over lies and cowardice…

For the nights are lonely and the road too long

For love is only for the lucky and strong…

This was beautiful once and now fading, bringing you down

That is how it works, voices around echo with a frown

Reasoning comes to play in defence

Without an answer to love, need or convenience…

Ever wondered why the butterfly goes to a particular flower?

Why does the peacock dance for the peahen in the first monsoon shower?

Why do leaves unquestioningly blow along with the autumn breeze?

Why do rivers joyously meet with the sea?

Love will arrive without notice like the changing season,

For it will make you happy for no reason…

Love has no reason, question or an answer stretching to infinity

From one everlasting moment to another, that's how it is meant to be.

- PaYal Jain

Love And Convenience

Have you ever fallen in love? Are you in love? Have you ever questioned why you are in love with someone? Are you tricking your mind with reasoning for the same? Are you in love with someone because they are beautiful, because they take care of you, because you get a feeling that makes you feel good? There is nothing wrong or right about feeling this way, but if you can rationalise love or ascribe it to sometime, you may be mistaking it for a long time.

You may like being with someone because of certain reasons, but you don't actually love someone for a reason. Loving someone is like having faith; you know that the reason is somewhere there, for it has to be, but it's too complex to figure out. The moment you think of love, it is always without a reason at that very moment, and then our so called sensible and reasonable mind comes into play with its logic props, submitting itself to the command of the character's role, only to invent reasons to satisfy that feeling of love or liking. Love keeps happening miraculously at all times and in all places, and can sustain itself without a defined reason, simply because it is meant to be. Love just happens without any explanation, notice or announcement.

Many of us at some point of our lives commit ourselves to someone, not out of love, but out of reasons fostered on protection, well-being, security, benefits and reassurance. We find love too intimidating and often give up on it, fearing the loss of control over our lives. We fear falling in love, and without even experiencing the power of that fall which could make us soar higher, we give up at the edge after climbing the cliff. Pause once in a while and look into your relationship. Ask yourself if you are in it for love or for convenience, does being in it makes you comfortable and at ease, or does it make you truly happy. Sometimes, we fail to gather the courage to answer the doubts and choose to live in denial, give in to our hearts playing tricks over whom to love and whom to not.

It is a myth that very few get lucky in love. The reality is that very few are able to align and choose love over comfort with all their heart and soul. The others who don't acknowledge these desires and are too afraid to follow their hearts and proclaimed unlucky. They settle for comfort over magic, cause over contentment, and convenience over love. Withdrawing from a relationship of convenience is scary for an unknown future that lies ahead, so we stick with it, compromising and settling, believing it to be what we deserve, tricking ourselves into staying. The reasons gratifying the poignant needs or finances are taken good care of, or the story between the sheets may be too good to be true, or walking down that uncertain road again terrifies us, so we stick to relationships that don't excite us completely. We're overcome by fear, yet we accuse love for its paucity.

We confine ourselves under obligations than experience love in its truest form. We are afraid of facing the societal judgements passed on the choice of our relationships. Studies reveal that people who stay in relationships of convenience for long struggle with anxiety and depression, have higher chances of suffering chronic diseases and their self-esteem plummets. If a relationship does not hold any meaning other than duties and chores, it is time to contemplate if that's the place you want to be in.

Have you ever wondered why the term 'making love' is used for sex? When you are in love, sex is indubitably incredible and truly fulfilling. It feels like a unique physical connection which no other can stimulate, like an extension of a physical union to a spiritual one, bringing close two souls pleasing each other in all possible manners. It is more than just a physically satisfying experience. It is only when we want to hold on to our convenience, yet wish to break free in search of love, that we misplace our trust in love.

Love and passion are either there or they aren't. Love is complete and whole in its own realm, not requiring any 'if's and 'but's. Even then, the conditioning steps in to make us settle for less, something that works as per the asserted societal norms. It will haunt you eventually, chain you in pretence while you mull over how you ended up there. Genuine love is above the need to be with someone. Sometimes you misjudge love with the needs, filling in the void in your life. It is a dangerous place to be in, sliced between need and the missing parts of the past. You will end up hurting yourself and the other person in the long run. We are conditioned to believe that love is something that your partner showers over you, an ingrained feeling of receiving it from a special someone. However, you are solely responsible for your feelings of joy and happiness. Trouble starts when we expect love to bring bliss. Love means to let the other person be and enjoy their presence, without expecting them to fill in the missing parts in us.

Even the ones in love can feel emotionally disconnected at times and misunderstand it for convenience. Voice your opinion and communicate your feelings. Pin your ears back and be receptive to the underlying emotions to bring back the love. If you commit yourself to love, you will see two separate beings sharing your individual journeys together, rather than feeling *one* on the *same journey*. There is great power in love that doesn't require someone's presence to confirm your joy and happiness. The presence just elevates the very feeling. The realisation of being in a relationship of convenience can take its toll on your mental well-being, but it is also a chance for you to confront your deeper issues and empower yourself to break the pattern. Your gut will tell you when things are going wrong, but don't shut it off with forceful rationalisation. It'll only weigh you down over time. There is no hard rule that once you are in love, you can't fall out of it. If it is meant to be, you will find millions of opportunities to fall back in love, deeper than ever before.

Being in love is scary and risky, but it surely is better than never risking anything, and never truly knowing what love is as a result.

The Changed Friendships

I think I am forgetting my friends' faces...

The conversations and hanging out at different places...

The laughter over jokes on daily chores...

Missing the gossip sessions, what's happening behind the doors...

I miss the talks and seeing the expressions...

Gauging, am I paying the bills 'cause I sense tension

I miss the road trips to destinations unknown...

Announcing I am heading to your place over the phone...

I miss the dine-outs and checking out the crowd...

The flirting, the attention game and friends' shout out...

I am missing the hugs and shoulder rubs

Sharing sadness inside, while eating from ice-cream tubs...

The friendships accuse and abuse...

The kicks, if I made us lose...

I am missing my first puffs...

Or the advice over life's roughs...

I don't see that connect anymore...

Analysing through their social profiles that roar...
It would be good to come out from those spaces...
Once in a while to meet up because
I think I am forgetting my friends' faces...

- PaYal Jain

The Friendship Amendments

I am nearing forty, and over the past two decades, my long time close friends have grown distant. At the same time, some strangers have turned out to be inseparable parts of me. It was confusing at first to see how friendships could easily be tossed aside, as it brewed doubts of middle-age crisis.

We all need friends in life, not for the joys or laughter alone that they bring, but to experience the bonding that keeps you alive for people outside your family and your aspirations. We need them to comprehend, connect, share, confess to and live with complete authenticity, for they don't question your being. We all need friends in our lives, for all intents and purposes, as much as we need air to breathe and food to eat. You may have hundreds of virtual friends closely observing your virtual social life, commenting on all your Instagram posts, but fail to be around to get you out of that slump. However, it is possible that you have outgrown these particular friends. Friends are like a backbone holding you strong, with your feet grounded and head held high. Though it's a fantastic feel and a pleasure to have lifelong bonds with friends, but the equation we share with some of them who accompanied us at different points of time in life might change. It is bound to happen, whether you blame it on age, time, circumstances, etc. Some friendships are meant to evolve with us, while some are just not meant to be.

Growing up, I often heard my mom say, "Your pals represent your own persona and thoughts." This expression always baffled me till I began meeting people while reflecting on who I was and what I was thinking at different points in my life. My childhood friends, friends made during college, through extracurricular activities, friends from our children's group or from work; they don't all accidentally bump into your life, but are the mirrors of our own persona. The laughter, the care and concern, the love we share, the secrets, and the ups and downs build an illusion of a lasting rock-solid relationship, but just like other human relationships, these bonds can also weaken and fade away. As we grow up and become more mature, our friendships aptly move on and change too.

As a young kid, I was always popular and had many friends of different ages, and always walked the extra mile to be there for them. I enjoyed spending time with them, even though I never had a set unchanging group of friends. My cousins were my friends with whom I played hide 'n' seek until wee hours of the night. I shared a friendly rapport with my seniors, for it was fun and cool to hang out with them. Mentoring juniors was also something I enjoyed. Being from a civilian family in an Army School, I tried to fit in and settle my friendships. I was into sports, which set me apart even more because most of the girls were not into it, so my love for sports costed me being laughed at and called names. However, defeating boys in the sports I liked taught me to handle unprecedented challenges, and the trail I left behind was an inspiration to many. I was friends with almost every popular person in school, yet I ended up keeping in touch with no one after passing out till Facebook brought us back in touch with each other. College ushered in new sets of friendships into my life. Post college, things changed again.

Friendships will always evolve. The friends you meet on your journey of life are God's or Nature's way of giving you support at that particular point of time, or teach you a lesson. Everyone has that special purpose. Sometimes, the one-time foes turn into your best friends, while you might sometimes get back in touch with an old friend and rekindle your friendship which you had thought you had moved on from. It might even be stronger than before because there might be something new to learn this time.

Friendships, whether lasting or over, are cherished forever. When you miss your friends, it is actually the moments spent with them and the feelings evoked that bring about the nostalgia. From sharing secrets to seeking advice, the uncontrollable laughter, the misunderstandings, sharing life's significant events — each of these moments help us row the boat of our lives. These relationships are like any other human relationships that go through ups and downs. Conflicts are normal to occur, but they can have lasting consequences, sometimes even ending the friendship.

Our lives are forever changing and that is one of the prime reasons why close friendships sometimes don't last. We move on with the events of our lives, get a new job, get married, have kids, move cities, suffer crises and so on. Some friendships can handle this change, while some of these changes become a wedge between friends, and they drift apart. Like in any other relationship, one needs to put in the effort, but not formality, to make a friendship work, nurture it with love and care, stand by the other when they need the additional backing. Real friendships comes with understanding and flexibility and they can say to each other, 'I am busy and I don't have time for you now,' and then go back to where they left off without the friendship being affected.

Real friendships fill you up with warmth and a sense of well-being. If you are suddenly feeling empty and being around your friends makes you feel belittled, it is time to move on. With self-reflection and increased wisdom comes the realization that divulges which relationships are meant to last and which are a passing phase. As in romantic relationships, some friendships are only good till they last. Most of us are yet to accept this dynamic. Relish these bonds, take pleasure in your friendships for what they are and till the time they are.

Looking back, you might recall these memories and smile. Take time and make the effort to rekindle some of these old friendships, strengthen the weakened ones and develop new ones. We are here on this earth for a limited time, so we should make the most of it to stay alive in the hearts of people long after we are gone.

Life And What Is Meant To Be

Often, life serves you with different thinking trails

To ascend or to fall, to choose your own way

To take the leap, to risk that plunge

To give your best shot, to take it off your lungs

For life never shies away from giving you chances

Take that call in your lows, when your journey is all tipsy dances

For it's the best time to judge your own capability

For it's the best time for the dares or raise to heights you reverie

To willingly let go and do what you were born for

Or is that too much to ask?

It's time to embrace that fear, that ridicule, that danger

Making you fall out of line with your comfort, boiling the anger

Time to endure in mediocrity

And let life be the way it was always meant to be.

- PaYal Jain

Are You Ready Enough?

Whether you prepare or not, you will never feel completely ready — ready for your first day at school, ready for commitments, ready to be a parent, ready for the death of a closed one. No one in the entire world is ever a 100 percent ready for anything until it comes about. You were safe in your mother's womb, in that small world of yours, then an unexpected hurly-burly caused you to show up in this world. You terrified, overwhelmed, in reverence of life, but never ready. The death of your parent from a long suffering disease might have prepared you for the inevitable, but when the time came, a surge of sorrow, remorse, and relief moved slowly into your heart, making you feel low, testing your preparedness. We humans are never ready and justify delay with this excuse. Readiness is a fib, a fabrication, a propaganda that we follow to delay action.

We all have moments in our lives wherein we may be prepared for a few things with a cautious awareness about the calculated unknowns, but you can never judge the moment precisely and feel all-the-way ready. We always feel that we could have practiced more, memorised the speech better before its delivery on stage at an important event, studied a little extra before sitting for the final exam, done more brain storming or research, asked for more opinions before taking up that project, saved a little more and be more sorted in our career before stepping into parenthood, and so on. Our 'could have's or 'more's will always be there. Five years from now, there will be new 'could have's. The truth is that you, in no way, can prepare yourself to board the train, feeling that the present one is too crowded. You'll simply end up waiting for another, then another, ultimately regretting taking the first one, inundated with remorse. If you don't dare to get on the train, you may lose out on the best chance to change your destiny forever. Even if the train is crowded, you will figure out your own balance and create a space for yourself. Taking the risk is better than regretting the chances you didn't take, or the moments you didn't seize.

Humans consider themselves to be safe and secure when they are in control, but life does not always go the way you plan it. It will often surprise you, elate you and dishearten you. There is no surety or certainty in life, besides death. We are just trapped in the vicious circle of fooling ourselves behind the flimsy veils of control, our feelings at the mercy of it. When things works in our favour, it feels great; otherwise, you boil up with fury and annoyance. If we continue our battle with control, we shall exhaust ourselves in defeat. Yet, we are curious to know what the future shall bring so that we are prepared enough to deal with it. This is not to say that planning and preparing is not important, for it would be ridiculous to expect things to just happen in your life, but we need to plan while also being open to unexpected results.

Bhagavad Gita: Chapter 2, verse 47 says:

कर्मण्येवाधिकारस्ते मा फलेषु कदाचन|

मा कर्मफलहेतुर्भूर्मा ते सङ्गोऽस्त्वकर्मणि||

karmaṇy-evādhikāras te mā phaleṣhu kadāchana

mā karma-phala-hetur bhūr mā te saṅgo 'stvakarmaṇi

It translates to the thought that you have a right to perform your prescribed duties, but you are not entitled to expect the good fruits of your actions. Never consider yourself to be the cause of the results of your activities, nor be attached to inaction.

Only action is in our hands, not the outcome. When we are worrying about the results, we become anxious for not meeting our own expectations. The fact is that when we are not affected by the outcome, we are proficiently reflecting on our own efforts in a much better way. When you learn to go with the flow, life becomes a little more easier than all your plans for it.

With the 'I'm just not ready' excuse, we express our terror and fear of the unknown. It is normal to feel this way, for we are scared to take the risk and dawdle in our safe known realms that don't challenge us. However, trust yourself when you take on a challenge to step into the unknown, trust that you will be able to make your own place there and learn. Life will challenge you now and then, testing your courage, and you will make mistakes and learn from them.

We are never prepared while growing up to deal with uncertainty, and only a few are able to navigate naturally through the unknown. The unexpected is inevitable, so be open, liberal and tolerant towards the unknown. Imagine yourself at a disco, dancing to the music being played. Each time the music changes, you manage to switch your dance moves and flow with the music instead of complaining about it. That is what the small lot does that lives happily. Dance to the rhythm of life and adjust your moves to the challenging tunes.

There will be moments in life when we will need to take a call to significantly shift the track of our lives and take on a drastic change. These moments might scare you at times, but they will lead you were you were always meant to be. Whenever there is an upheaval in your life, it is a sign that a change is due. It is an opportunity for you to learn what you are seeking. Believe in taking these chances, even if it questions your sanity. You might not be able to see where the train is taking you, but things will start to change once you decide to get on the train. Listen to your inner voice, it will make everything fall into place. Give yourself a chance and allow yourself to fail. You will always question whether you are ready or not. Well, are you?

Regrets

Sometimes, the heart sinks in regrets
For the mistakes you have made
For passing the wrong choice's gate
For the roads you have travelled
For the hurts and the gravels
For cheating on your soul
For pretending to fit in a role

You wish to travel time and fix them all
To stop the uneasiness caused by the regret ball
To free from being frozen and powerless
Free from feeling small while shattering the burden of regret
To shut all the thoughts of guilt in a sudden moment

It's not too late to start now
Without bothering with the 'how'
Maybe the beginning can't be revisited and changed
Time to be more aware and compassionate
For the magic wand — God did not send
Start now and change the end.

- PaYal Jain

Sinking In Guilt

We all go through a time in our lives when we feel remorseful, ashamed and regretful for the mistakes made in the past. We start feeling guilty and sink in the same. At times, we are able to pull ourselves out of the guilt trap, but often we are just torn apart by the feelings of this guilt. Regret is a form of self-punishment for being wrong in the past, for doing something that shouldn't have been done, for making the wrong choices, for saying things that shouldn't have been said, etc. This guilt trap starts to spread its claws around us, suffocating us to the core. We start living everyday of our lives fitting in the roles and hoping no one finds out our wrongdoings from the past.

We cannot undo the past or change the things we are not very proud of, but we can choose to not be the prisoners of past. Regretting the deeds done in the past will do no good, but dwelling on the lessons of not repeating the same mistakes will. All of us make mistakes, but it takes a lot of courage and character to know you're wrong, and to be able to own and mend it. The only thing that does not allow us to be courageous is pride, for it takes this acceptance as a weakness.

It takes guts and humility to admit your mistakes, to put your past behind you and look towards the future takes courage, coming out of the 'what if' to 'what is possible' takes courage. Once a mistake is over, it is no more a reality for you. Don't get stuck there or let it define you. You always have the choice to make things right from the present onwards and shape your future. While you do so, knock down the fear and the pride inhibiting you.

God has not given any of us the magic wand to turn back time and undo our wrong doings, but it won't matter if you choose now to be a compassionate and loving being, and decide to treat people with consideration and thoughtfulness. It is never too late to begin again, forgetting the person you were and remembering the person you want to be.

If you look back now, you might be ashamed of some of the things you did in the past — treated someone miserably, stole for your self-interests, intentionally plotted against someone, hurt someone that bad that it changed their life forever, cheated on your spouse and so on. It is impossible to go back and change what you did, no matter how badly you wish to. The deed is done and is engraved as a choice in your life forever, but the choice to beat yourself up over it or let go also lies with you. Imagine if Saint Valmiki was stuck in self-loathing, he would never have been the man he became later. Saint Valmiki was once Ratnakar, a murderer and a robber. In a robbery encounter with Narada once, Narada asked him if his family, for whom he had chosen the path of robbery and merciless killing, would share the sins he is committing. Ratnakar was sure of the fact that his family would, but on confronting them, none of the family members agreed to bear the burden of his sins. It was in that moment that he understood that no one pays the price for your sins, and no one can change the reality for you either. It is you and only you who can do what you set your heart and soul to.

It was this realization within Angulimala after meeting Buddha that turned him into an arahant (a monk). The short tempered King Ashoka became a Buddhist and a peace propagator after the war of Kalinga.

In 1991, Shaka Senghor, a young drug dealer with a quick temper and a semi-automatic pistol, shot and killed a man. He says it was not the end of his story, but the beginning of acceptance, apology and amends. For a long while, he did not take responsibility for his actions and blamed everyone except himself, rationalizing his decision to shoot. It was then a letter from his son that changed his life and served as a ray of light to illuminate the dark place he was in. The words in that letter made him introspect and he knew he was a changed man. His transformation began with this realization, he challenged himself over his decisions in life, he read about poets, authors and philosophers. During his time in prison, he read Malcolm X's autobiography and shattered every stereotype he had about himself. It was then that he started maintaining a journal, writing his experiences during childhood and his times in prison. He did apologise for his actions and in response, one of the relatives of his victim told him that she forgave him. It was in that moment that he felt open to forgiving himself. He started sharing his experiences and realized that everyone had had a past that made them do what they did, so he started doing everything in his power to help change that. His experience shows that we have a fair chance of redeeming our acts most times, through first acknowledging the hurt, apologising not for others to forgive you, but to feel right, and most importantly, liberating yourself and becoming one with yourself.

Sooner or later in our lives, we will do things we will regret. Regret is an indicator that the lesson is learned and you surely are a changed person. If life throws same curveballs at you now, you would not react the way you did in the past. The bad decisions thus help you in some way or the other in becoming the person you are today. Reflect on your mistakes and learn. We all have the potential to be divine or devilish, and it all depends on our awareness of our body, vigour, mind, and understanding at that moment within all of us. To be aware of the possibility of knowledge and erudition may be awakened any moment that makes people be the best versions of themselves. Changing the beginning is not possible, but there is always the possibility to change the end if we create the space for it to happen–a space where we refuse to be held hostage by our past misdeeds and mistakes, and not let that define us for the rest of our lives.

Insecurities

Chained in the bonds of insecurity locked deep within
Abandoned in the hypocrite and judgemental society we live in
Giving in to the voices, acting upon lies and excuses
While ignoring the truth, indulging in the abuses
Will I ever break free from the this insecurity slavery?
Will I accept me as I am with all bravery?

The self-doubts once created have chosen to stay
Dismissal suffocates within, yet the price I continue to pay
Mastered the art of cheating myself in the process
The shaming voice slurring what I possess
Will I ever come out of fear's darkest corner?
Will I ever be able to prevent being a bleak mourner?

I have failed to accept me, I confess
My truth in shackles, I fail to express
The insecurity knot is tightening its grip
My verity startled, scared to strip
Lord, help me, love me with my imperfections,
Let me overcome my insecurities, tapping my own connection.

- PaYal Jain

Hiding Under Lies And Excuses

We all feel insecure from time to time and put our insecurities across in various ways. These expressions depend upon our beliefs, nature, conditioning, and everything whittled by our own experiences. In some, these feelings will reflect as weakness or passivity, while in others it may be seen as their daring, toughness, and vivacity. When insecure, some may be seeking attention while others may be avoiding it completely. If we were on the terrace of a high storied building and found the railing to be broken, we would feel insecure nearing it. Or if we were driving by a disturbed militancy affected area, we certainly would feel insecure. Insecurities walk in as forewarnings, signalling the presence of danger, and warn us to prepare appropriately. Insecurity coming out of circumstantial fears warns, but we often don't deal with these warnings and it becomes a state of our being. It slowly then crawls in to deplete our self-confidence, indices a fear of rejection or a strange sense of inferiority.

We all have some monsters within us. These vague qualms and worries hold us back in many ways, making us insecure about our relationships, our financial status, etc., forming patterns in our lives.

You didn't reply to my text? It couldn't possibly be because you did not receive it or it accidentally got deleted. *You are ignoring me! You didn't respond to my invitation?* It couldn't possibly be because you have not seen it yet as you are still in shock of seeing your blood test reports cueing immediate medical assistance. You are simply ignoring me!

These insecure patterns are so deeply ingrained in us, put in by a series of events bolstering and reinforcing this state of being. In all of us lies emotions that prodigiously sculpt our self-image and manipulate our behaviour. These insecure emotions bring about ceaseless waves of worry and critical thoughts. Reflect on your life and ask yourself, "Did your insecurities fire up with someone else's actions or words?" You will be surprised to realise that the greater part of your insecurities was imbued in you by others while you accepted them to be your own state of being.

We human are social creatures, and thus intend to be sociable and likeable. However, we mistake the two to be the same. In the process, we fall into that trap of believing that we're not good enough or less. We let these validations and approvals form a pattern of escapism from our real identities, while being knocked down by insecurities which try to warn us about the dangers to our identity. When these validations threaten our sense of identity, it is a warning telling us something about our real being. Silencing that voice then weighs us down and makes us feel vulnerable. We have insecurities for a reason, which is to address that silenced voice which is asking us to look into the various aspects to improve within ourselves.

Our insecurities can make us feel on our nerves all the time. We might believe that we are not liked, we don't fit in, we will be left alone, we will have financial issues, and the list goes on. It makes us act in ways that we sometimes feel ashamed of, and has the ability to impair us in outrageous ways. We so feel embarrassed by the way these insecurities make us feel that we hide them with lies and excuses, fearing judgemental opinions. However, we're only making a fool of ourselves about keeping them locked deep within. The irony of the whole situation is that people do see through these lies and react to your phony projection, often leaving you feeling even more insecure.

We all know in our heart of hearts our real self. Our real entity has all the answers to what we truly love, desire, and believe in. We just don't ask the questions and deal with the insecurities for they confer on us a temporary relief. That is the reason why avoidance and blaming get under way of dealing with these flaws. These insecurities are signs laid on the lines of your real identity, giving an inkling of a true self being challenged or a false credence finally bare. We choose to avoid rather than examine the naked truth, the worst fears about ourselves.

Feeling insecure is inevitable. You might have been told, 'You're good for nothing', 'You are such an ugly person', 'You don't deserve love', 'You will never be successful', and these 'you are…' statements grew in your head and it adapted to its tone. We may grow shy, pull back from relationships, projecting these attacks into our actions towards our loved ones. Think of a life where you could free yourself of these imposed insecurities.

Even the most happy and confident people feel insecure at times. There is a lot of stigma attached to insecurities when it comes to self-love. It is believed that one can't feel insecure if one loves the self. Going by my own experience, I can say that you may love every cell in your body but still have insecurities, or might want to change certain aspects of oneself. As humans, we are constantly changing. Call it anxiety or inhibition or self-doubt, it is a universal part of all humans.

It is okay to feel down at times, angry or jealous at others, fearful and irrational to some extent. We only need to remember that these insecurities are living inside, and the more we feed them, the stronger they will grow. That does not imply dismissing their existence altogether. When we silence these insecurities out of fear, we give them power over us and our actions. It is time to listen to these voices and embrace not only the apparent imperfections, but also the way they make you feel. It involves untangling the identity knot before it begins to tighten and trap the self in doubts. These insecurities are actually the dwindling violets underpinning this beautiful bouquet of humanity, for it leads to self-awareness, walking with our heads held high, living with authenticity with an open and trusting heart. When light is shone onto an insecurity, it suddenly begins to fade by itself, leaving nothing but an actual secure feeling.

"When you are content to be simply yourself and don't compare or compete, everyone will respect you."

— Lao Tzu, Tao Te Ching

Falling Apart

You stand there on the uncertain threshold of breath
Like a wary stranger ambiguous of your knowledge
The many attempts ravaged by time's tortuous winds
Drowning you in a whirlpool of sorrows
You act when the Earth gapes and swallows it all
And now you mock as you rock to and fro
Bemused, clapping your blood stained hands
Incessantly, eternally like the one possessed
And then you suddenly stop
Like a magician, you create again
An ephemeral illusion benevolently
And all that fallen apart stir
Rise to all that is worth living for
You are worth, really you are…

- PaYal Jain

Smashed Down

Sometimes we do not see it coming and we arrive at a place in life where we are bereaved of everything we once had. How could your marriage fall apart? Or your career be doomed? Maybe you made a foolish mistake or have been irrational lately, or are simply unlucky. The reasons don't change the reality of your life being a complete mess, leaving you crumbled and confused over how to pick up these pieces together. Looking at these pieces, you torture and punish yourself in a myriad ways. We all have had hard times in life where we are so lead on with thoughts of dejection, darkness and sadness, and become numb with the helplessness of being this way, completely fallen apart with frustrations and dissatisfaction. It hurts and no one understands, because no one is experiencing the pain tearing us apart.

We find it difficult to accept the pain and are unable to draw a parallel between this change and the comfort threatening our survival. Nothing in life stays static, making things spin out of control once in a while. We often fail to manoeuvre life ahead, yet survive it. It does not kill us, but only makes us stronger. Ever wondered why? Because when things get wrecked and ruined, there lies a gateway of opportunity waiting to be realized.

Do you believe that there are people living on this planet leading perfect lives with no struggles at any point of their lives at all? We all are going through our own churns and struggles. We all live through grief, heartbreaks, disappointments, sufferings and vulnerability. There is no escape and no exception, and the pain felt is more or less the same. Life is never perfect, never was and never will be for anyone, because certain aspects are bound to collapse after they have served their purpose in our life. If the pieces did fall apart, it is all together an opportunity to put these pieces back together in an entirely new manner. This lock, stock and barrel configuration of your life helps you to create a stronger foundation that buoys you up and help you grow. When you hit life's worst, it is time to hold yourself while gathering all the strength to keep pushing yourself onwards.

There are no more than two kinds of individuals when it comes to living through the worst; one who hit rock bottom, cry and get stuck there forever, and the others who pull themselves together and bounce back with the knowledge that underneath that pain lies resilience, adaptability and capacity to survive. When things fall apart, which they will now and then, do remember that it is the time when you can either flounder in your fall or rise up from it.

When things fall to bits, it tears us apart and beats us down with hopelessness, threatening our security and stability. The universe exists because everything was taken away once only to transport through the journey of creation. The existence is entropic in a beautiful manner. The universe came to be from a central point which expanded outwards, falling out of that concentrated core into diverse materializations, including the Earth and other planets, galaxies, stars, and so on. It's an irony that the universe is a beautiful creation of its core falling to pieces. Life also functions by breaking down the core for creating and recreating.

Staying optimistic when your world has fallen apart is easier said than done, yet when it passes, you know that it happened for you to be able to turn your life around, fair or unfair — whichever way you may perceive it. Every situation in life is as miserable as one's outlook towards it. Life itself is never fair or unfair, it simply happens to be the way it is.

Many find themselves mourning over their adversities and hardships, seeking a Godly explanation to their condition, questioning their luck and deeds that made them entitled to the believed punishments. It is no punishment. Sometimes, the worst things happen to the best of the lot and you can't go on beating yourself up for the same.

When you hit rock bottom, the only place you can go is up. Accept the aspect that fell apart, admit that the foundation crumbled and no longer supports you. Whether that foundation was a person you loved or a career you built over years, know that it is no longer there in your life. What you thought was right for you wasn't giving you a chance to explore what actually is. You need not have to have all the answers at that moment. All you need is to take a step away and onwards.

"Life mysteriously falls into place even when at first it seems utterly falling apart, for things fall apart to fall back into place just as the little seed knows that to sprout, it needs to be thrown out in the dirt, enclosed in the dark and thrash about to reach to light."

Nothing At All

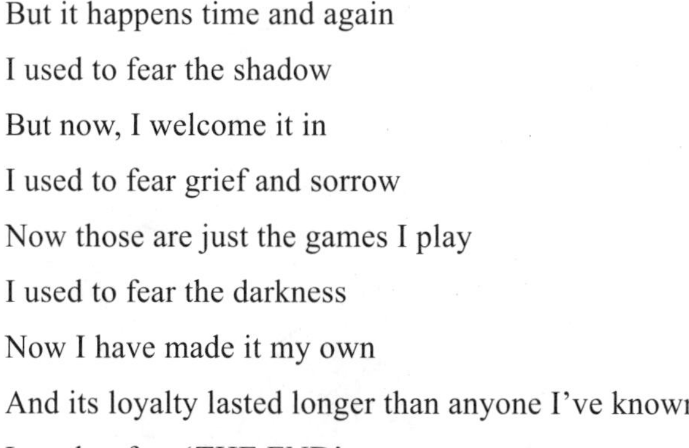

I used to fear a broken heart
But it happens time and again
I used to fear the shadow
But now, I welcome it in
I used to fear grief and sorrow
Now those are just the games I play
I used to fear the darkness
Now I have made it my own
And its loyalty lasted longer than anyone I've known
I used to fear 'THE END'
Now that fear has ceased
Destroy what is still left of me
And give my soul some peace
I say I accomplish a lot, causing many fears to fall
But heart, just between you and me
I have accomplished nothing at all

- PaYal Jain

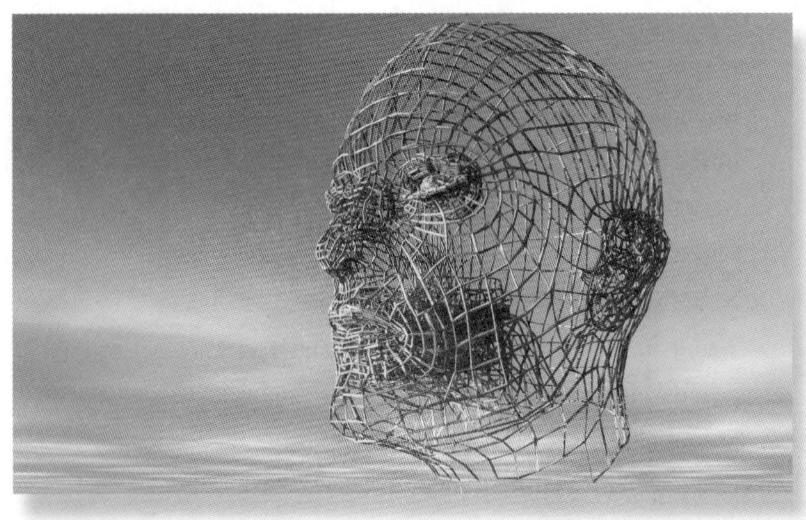

Emptiness Inside

Many people go through this quandary, the dilemma in life, where they are cleft stick with having everything in life including financial abundance, a successful career, a healthy relationship and a loving family, and the entire opulence of comforts they ever wished for, yet feel empty inside. You may call it mid-life crisis, the blues, depression, downturn, gloominess or other names that signify a hollowness inside and can feel very upsetting.

Lately, Michael Phelps, the most acclaimed and recognised Olympian swimmer who has 23 gold to his medal tally, came out and acknowledged his depression and suicide anticipation. Who would have thought that after being the most successful Olympian ever, he was considering taking his own life? Robbin Williams, the legendary actor known for his comic excellence took his own life at the age of 63, for he could not live with the crisis inside him anymore. There are many celebrities from all arenas who are now opening up about their depression. Jim Carrey said in one of his interviews, "I think everybody should get rich and famous and do everything they ever dreamed of so they can see that it's not the answer."

As humans we are always looking for more and chase riches, success and fame, while searching for happiness, and even after having it all, there is no sense of fulfilment. We want more and are never completely appeased because having it all does satiate the want, but reinforces the tendency to strive for even more while feeling less. When you buy a new car, it is an amazing feeling initially, but then it is just a car which you would willingly sell off or trade away in a few years when you get bored of it. Materialism, fame, wealth, etc. will quickly bore you once you have had it for a while, and you will come back to the feelings you had before you had all that. You will then realise that all this was nothing but a short-term happiness rush.

We humans are conditioned to venerate happiness, whatever it is as per our beliefs and conditioning. A beautiful house, a sports car, a fat balance in the bank account — whatever the parameter of being happy is, we have it and then start to curtail and cut it down, only to feel the conflicting opposite. We camouflage it while wearing the mask of happiness. In the process of proving our wellbeing to the world, we become voiceless and shy away from baring our true emotions. The masks may vary keeping up the illusion propagated by the conditioned world and publicized by the social media, whilst the dilemma crawls inside like fungus, throttling and strangling you.

The world around us demands us to be happy in a particular way, and when you match the societal criteria ruled by its demands, you may not feel this way anymore. Then, when you are faced with the question, "Why are you so low?" you feel confused for you don't have an answer. It's like questioning somebody suffering from cancer the reason for them being ill, sick and tired. You have no answer to the questions of feeling dead inside, feeling worthless and being affected by nothing and everything; you have no answer to feeling cold or emotionless, then feeing overwhelmed with gushes of emotions that leave you helpless with a soul-wrenching void.

By hiding your true feelings or running away from the melancholy or pretending its nonexistence, you are confirming it to commit a crime. The guilt drives many people to the edge. Most of them don't want to die, but they feel intolerably and agonizingly stuck and tired of carrying on the 'everything is fine' mask. They want someone to pull them back, yet want nobody to know their weaknesses. They project the image of perfection to the outside world, irrespective of the venomous storm tearing them down within.

You are frightened and ashamed to open up because you do not want to be judged by the stigmas attached to mental well-being. You do not want to be perceived as a failure, so you choose to suffer in silence. Eventually, this torture, this conflict, grows to be uncontrollable and you resort to self-destructive methods to shrink the suffering. The less you talk about it, the more ashamed you will be of your feelings, of your questionable contemplations. Something is definitely missing here. It could be someone's presence, something you wanted but couldn't attain. Are you missing your partner's affection, or having a partner at all? There is only one thing that truly fills the soul, and that is Love. The dearth of love presents itself in the form of nonexistence of a connection within, triggered off rejection and abandonment. Ignoring your feelings and judging yourself renders your core weak and manoeuvres shame for being flawed towards it.

Don't be hard on yourself for simply being human. We all should embrace the complexity of life and struggling at our own pace. Gloominess or melancholy is part of that complex story, and you yourself give it the power to meddle with your existence. According to WHO's latest reports from 2015 on depression and anxiety, people living with depression worldwide are around 322 million. There is no indignity in accepting that you are feeling dreadful inside. In fact, it takes more courage than many people can ever imagine. Finding that courage to own your weaknesses, and do not allow it to overpower you.

The world we live in, with its growing chaotic pace, the pressures are endless and we are more likely to go into such despair with a trifling vexation, putting our mental well-being at stake. As long as we are able to deal with it, it is acceptable, but when we are not, anxiety and depression cause our life to come crashing down and affects our mental well-being. Besides, we are under the scrutiny of the world judging us for our way of handling life. Why is it not okay to deal with it like we deal with a cold or cough? Why is talking about it such a taboo, when global communication can happen at the speed of light? Why don't families and friends come in support when such things are triggered in us? Why can't we stop the blame game and actually work on mental well-being at large?

Remember that we do have an unbelievable strength within; we just have to embrace it. Don't let the societal norms weigh down our sense of fulfilment. These bouts of emptiness are lessons, signs and reminders of our life's true purpose. Don't be afraid of the ghost of doubt deeply rooted within you. Stop caring for what others think and start caring about how you feel. When you undress the layers of phony exhilaration, you are bound to get hurt. But along with this pain comes the freedom to be and to do things. Forgive yourself and be grateful for the blessings in your life. We tend to miss out on things we already have — the joy of laughing with friends and family, relishing a meal, staying humble, being kind, the connection within, and all the other things that feel like a whole nine yards of struggle, are the ones that makes you rich in experience.

The ultimate goal is to live through these experiences of life to their fullest potential. Break free from the trap of feeling lesser, feeling empty, and recreate yourself. When you align the you with the 'you' that you seek to be, the emptiness will start to fill itself with a sense of fulfilment.

Me & My Life

The inner storm brings us out to the edges
Questions of existence take over
A callous run from self-exploration
Smashed by the meaning of life
And then you discover life is like a kaleidoscope
Always on the move but not repeats
Diverse patterns and ever changing transitions
Like the moments in our lives
And just a few of them justify your existence
Just like the captures in the kaleidoscope hold the draw for you
It is the joy of falling in love for the first time
Watching the sunset and cry
Holding the hand of your child for the first time
You look back at these moments and smile
Just the way you enjoy the flamboyant captures
And not the power of the kaleidoscope making it happen

It’s the moments and the transitions which will make life
And not the other way round...

- PaYal Jain

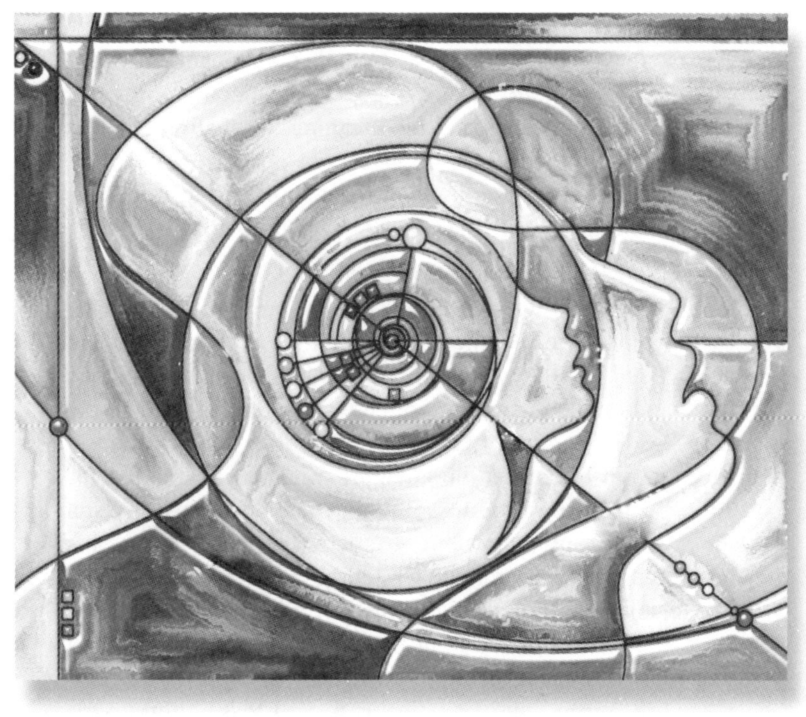

The Meaning Of My Living

Who am I? What is the meaning of my existence? What is my purpose? What is the meaning of life? We all are faced with such questions probing our purpose, our existence and the meaning to our living. I was also among the many looking for an answer, wandering, yearning for a purpose, looking for certain and firm reasons that I could lean upon and find my own calling in life.

Things don't just randomly come up. I was going through a period where I was struggling for my purpose and was hit by the intensity of the meaning of life. My son was six when he asked me, "Ma, what is life?" How could I have answered the question the answer to which was so confounded in my own head? Tapping my conscious faculties for a response, I asked him back what he knew of 'life'. I was looking for an answer for myself, but nothing came. Now I had my son looking up to me with hope, expecting an answer from his hero then. I held my tongue while I paid attention to what he had to say and all of a sudden, the storm inside settled down. He said he was not sure, but life was something within him that made him feel alive. In an instant, I knew I had been asking the wrong question all this time. I kissed him on his forehead and told him that he was right, *what keeps you alive is what life is*.

For a long time, I was looking for something conclusive to call it the purpose of my existence. I even attended some expensive workshops that assured me a rendezvous with my purpose, but even more confused I was when done, as I still did not know the answer. I was seeking the meaning of my life only to realise that this was not the question to be answered in the first place, but a simple clarity challenging me to question my aliveness; to reason it in my own articulations. Looking into a realm of mirrors at different points of your life, you will discover that your purpose is to explore the aliveness for yourself from start till the end.

The meaning of life has always been there right in front of me, so evident and so simple. It is to solely be alive. Even then it made me run around, losing my nerves looking for something concrete. Knowing what makes me alive and why it does so, a lot of questions did get answered. Things that excited me, that brought a smile to my face and that let me lose myself were different purposes at different point of time in my life. Even if I was not sure of the ultimate reason, I knew that I had to step into the reconnaissance of my life and relish the experiences of this journey.

"The two most important days in your life are the day you are born and the day you find out why."

— Mark Twain

Chasing your 'why's transforms the whole thing. Your aliveness is ever changing, and that is the reason why you cannot put a time-frame around it. Discovering what truly matters in a moment gives the reason for you to be alive in that moment. Exploring what keeps you alive will align you with your 'why's and elucidate the meaning behind your existence in that moment. *Right now* is the time to comprehend and get involved in things that genuinely matter. The more meaningful our thoughts and actions are, the more positivity and joy shall be begot to placate the purpose.

The meaning is not hiding outside of us that we have to go search for. It is neither some phenomena looming to be encountered, nor a miraculous transformational moment that will alter your life forever. Meaning is something we continue to introspect and bring to light. What is important today was not significant yesterday and might not be of great consequence tomorrow. The meanings will change; the 'what' and the 'why' aspects of being alive must be strived for and replenished constantly and persistently while aligning actions into the same.

Humans are driven by meaning and events, and it is the association between these events that has an effect on the experience. Meaning drives us and puts us into action. When there is a meaning that holds significance, one will go to insane lengths to make things happen. Flip through the pages of any war, any religious belief, family concerns, etc., people often go to the extent of giving up their lives for conferring meaning upon their associations. When you understand what keeps you alive, you start attributing sense to even the tiniest things you do and start connecting the dots to accomplish a greater purpose, for the most rousing and stirring choices are ones that ally with your 'why'.

When you seek the meaning of being alive, you open yourself to possibilities that challenge youto pursue something of greater significance. The truth of the matter is that you have every breath of your life to figure out and learn what it means to be you. The answers will keep on changing and so will the experiences. The moment you feel you have an answer, life will present a different question. Whether you answer it or not is irrelevant. What matters is getting up and facing the question as many times as possible and create answers for it.

मंज़िल तो तेह कर,
रास्ता भी मिल जाएगा।
चलना तो शुरू कर,
कारवां भी बन जाएगा।
होंसला तो बुलंद कर,
उमीदों का आसमान भी झुक जाएगा।
ख्वाब सी इस ज़िन्दगी में कुछ तो कर गुजर ,
मिलेगा सुकून और खुदा भी झुक जाएगा।

–पायल जैन

Translation: Get clear about your goals and you will find the way. Start moving in that direction and everything will fall into place. Keep your drive and morale intact and the skies of hope will fall to your knees. Start working towards the life of your dreams, you will be at peace while the Lord and the universe will conspire to make it happen for you.

Many confuse the meaning with ascertaining goals for themselves. They want the big house, fancy cars, feature amongst the top 10 influencers of the world, and so on. It gives them a reason to look forward to every day. But then at the same time, these goals can engender vacuity and bring along emptiness, once achieved. Contradictorily, the meaning or the purpose has no substance for there is no goal. The meaning must bring perpetual contentment and peace.

We are privileged to be alive at this moment. Whether it is a part of God's plan or not to give us a purpose, we should ask ourselves what meaning we want to be remembered for, and strive to create our own purpose. Life did not come with a congealed explanation for any one of us, and each of us has a different definition for it, like our own perspectives. Our journeys are different, our paths are separate but we all do have one common destination that we cannot escape — death. Yet, most people are not going to die because they never truly live in the first place.

"Live as if you were to die tomorrow. Learn as if you were to live forever." -Mahatma Gandhi

Pull out all the stops and strive to live in a manner you want to be remembered by. Let your acts and legacy pen down the words for the world to read after you're gone. It is beautiful the way we choose to give life a meaning, and find out why we are here while we are.

How Deep Is Your Love

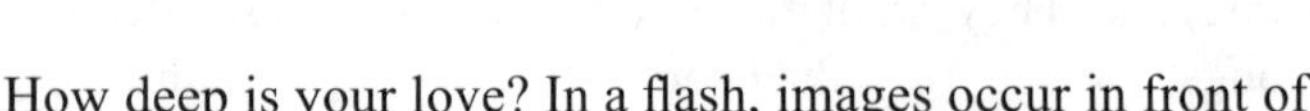

How deep is your love? In a flash, images occur in front of your eyes,

Some fulfilled promises and some hurt of the lies…

Some caring gestures that may have melted your heart,

Some romantic walks or eating corn by the cart…

Those endless conversations spent in silence,

Those passionate kisses and those moments, so intense…

How deep is your love? Straight away, making you smile in pride…

And for those who don't call themselves lucky in love may want to hide…

Rating the answer from low to high, bolstering fealty or do I sense a sigh?

How deep is your love with yourself on special days or every day?

Abruptly, you never thought of it, or said your say…

When did you hold yourself fulfilling your purpose in life?

Or were you too busy and lost in the self-strife…

Wrapping the answer in excuses of responsibility or practicality,

Turning your back on your needs, your self-esteem, in the cloak of lucidity…

Take a trip to visit the beauty inside you, and be someone who makes you feel loved,

You carry so much love for others; don't you think some of it needs to be rubbed...

What is your latest relationship status with the self?

Maybe, it's time to look at life's Delph

For you have cried or gotten over your relationships with others that did not match your score,

But did you even pass when the answer is around the person you live eternally with for sure?

Begin the romance with the self, for that's the relationship that's going to last forever

And when it comes to loving yourself, don't you say *never* ever…

LOVE YOURSELF! LOVE LIFE!

-PaYal Jain

Falling In Love With Self

Take some time off and sneak a quick look on your relationship with yourself on a day-to-day basis. If you had been another person, how would you have been at being in a relationship with you?

Before that sinks in, ask yourself an honest question and answer it with even more integrity. If you had to score between one to ten the degree of love that you hold for yourself, what would your score be?

I was asked the same question in one of the classes I attended and shared my score of perfect ten, only to get incongruous looks form the fellow attendees. I soon began to get a handle on my professed image of a selfish and an egocentric being, which changed by the end of the course by the way, yet my score remained unchanged. This score was not always a perfect ten.

Most of us when hit by the question — whom do you love the most, answer by naming many others except ourselves. Is it not strange that we keep ourselves way down below our spouse/lover, children, friends who apropos all hold the power to make us go weak or may leave us at their own will? On the contrary, the one that stays with us till the end and continues to be by our side through the different realms of life is loved the least by us.

All our lives, we are taught to believe that having meaning in life is being able to be useful to or in the world, to be able to contribute, mostly in relation to other people. Everything is under scrutiny all the time. Not doing a job or taking a break from one does not imply 'having no life'. People who are mostly by themselves are constantly viewed as boring and nerdish. People with odd interests are the non-important ones among peers, even if the said individuals are the most talented ones.

In spite of holding talent uniquely, we go by the judgements of the outside world. Being compared, we feel small or gargantuan, feeding the self to dwell in sadness or pride, wrapped all the while in self-doubt. We buy in lies, knowingly or unknowingly, from parents, teachers, friends, and others, and let them fool around with our self-esteem. Conventional images of inflated perfection create doubts around our own unique qualities delineated in the world within.

We are so obsessed with perfection that we overlook the fact that if all falls in contours of the same, everything around will be similar, monotonous and very boring. It is the little so called imperfections in each one of us that makes us stand out and this uniqueness in millions in the world makes this planet such a beautiful place.

Trapped in the 'perfect' image set by others, we become insecure of our own imperfections we crave for the bodies flashing on screen, we want the muscle cars and deep down feel small about the mismatch of us and the perfect metaphors out there, as if we aren't perfect the way others are. Good or bad, news is that no one on this earth is actually seamlessly unflawed. When you build an image of yourself in a certain way, your mind fools around to validate the same.

Remember for a moment the best moment of your life, the instance when all eyes were on you and everyone was raving about your success. How did you feel? Did it lift you up to cloud nine and were you in love with everything about yourself? What then when the opposite happens? Do you like yourself when you fail in exams or gain a few inches around your waist? Do you like yourself when you are not able to bring the greens and meet the ends? In despair then, we just judge ourselves by the parameters set by the society. If things go our way, we shower ourselves with love and reward ourselves for putting the right foot forward. But what when things go the other way round, we transpire callousness and become too hard on ourselves.

Self-love is accepting who we are and loving that person unconditionally. When was the last time you truly did something for yourself, or how frequently do you do the same? Fearing being considered selfish, we limit our love to remain only for others! In the process, we just stop living for ourselves, putting our personal happiness at the bottom of our priority list. But when we don't live up to the expectations of our loved ones, we start belittling ourselves.

Self-love is putting your needs first, and it's not entirely selfish to want the same. Caught between personal, professional, and a zillion other things, we tend to neglect the things we find joy in. The social stereotypes of having a successful career, a loving and supporting family, a caring partner and so on do not always compensate for our inner peace, making us feel narked and unhappy. It is only when we are at peace with the person we are without contradictions in our mind, that we get comfortable in our skin and spirit. We then become more open to love, and our loving ourselves and others gains a new meaning. Self-love is being true to your own feelings and choosing to act upon the same, while also taking responsibility for all our actions.

When on an airplane, you are advised to put on your own oxygen mask before you help others; it's kind of the same thing with love. The more you embrace self-love, the more aware you become of your feelings as well as those of others. When you don't rely on sources outside for love, it makes you more comfortable within. It is in your hands how loved you wish to make yourself feel. Go take those bubble baths, get the fancy facial treatments, or embark upon solo trips if that makes you happy. Do it, but know that there is more to self-love than just pampering yourselves. Do not bequeath your energies or neglect your own needs, giving away the key to your happiness to someone else. The strength it takes to truly appreciate ourselves is one that is rarely acknowledged by those around us.

"You can search throughout the entire universe for someone who is more deserving of your love and affection than you are yourself, and that person is not to be found anywhere. You yourself, as much as anybody in the entire universe, deserve your love and affection."

— Buddha

Beauty In Here And Now

Are you living life as it happens?

Are you beating yourself down with time cannons?

Entangled in the thoughts of the future or worries of the past…

Letting this moment slip and the now to pass

Wrapped in intoxicating, hallucinogenic masks of deceptions

Perfectly presenting the illusion of time's reflections…

And here, the *now* always struggles for a define ploy

While the race to be in the global virtual world makes life a toy…

Are you walking back into the past?

Or busy creating a thing in the future?

When did you last sit back and relax, not looking for shadows

Awakening the seed of life to unveil what's beneath the hollows…

For life is now in the simple smiling and feeling whole

For life is now in the kindling of your own soul
For life is now, rising in the falls
For life is now in the willing call

Are you willing to take off the mask of deception?
Ready to leave the illusion of time and the materialist reflection?
To seize the day and live in the moment
Leaving the then or will be atonement
Feel the moment and, like others, this will pass too
Not changing or coming back and yet haunting you...
Live it before it is a memory to look back
No matter if it brings a smile or an emotional sack...

Are you willing to live in the here and now?
Are you willing to let go wondering how?
Live to be you for the rest are taken for sure...
Nothing in the sham for nothing it cures
And when it's time to go and all the moments flash
You are not ready to leave with this inner clash
For you did not cry when you should have cried
For you did not live truly before you died...

Are you set to rise above the illusionary expectations?
Prepared to come out of struggling complications?
Let go of the moments once you've lived them fully
And not let them linger and play the bully
Free yourself of wandering thoughts
Free yourself of the body-mind disharmony knots
Let the may or may have been not make you saddened
For life is beautiful as it happens…

- PaYal Jain

Life As It Happens

How often do you find yourself wandering in the past or the future, beating yourself up with guilt, worry, regret, unfulfilled hopes and aspirations? We cannot completely free ourselves of either of these time realms, for the past not only brings guilt and regret, but also first-hand experience; and though future is driven by fears, it also brings along hope for the realisation of dreams. But if you pin your ears back to these thoughts, you would realise that the sensations and emotions drawn from the past or future affect the present and take you away from living in the moment.

With dominant influences of the past and the future, is it even possible to live in the moment? The moment is so transitory that the future becomes past so soon without the present being recognised. We might have developed means to register time in terms of seconds, minutes and hours, but in life, we experience time in a very different way. Engaging time spent with friends flees by in a flash, while even a few minutes spent at a boring engagement feel like hours. Sometimes, a day stretches on to eternity, while some days pass by with the blink of an eye. The present is measured by your action or engagement, and your awareness of the same. Most times, we work on an 'autopilot' mode, carrying out our daily chores without even without even registering our actions — whether it is gulping food down the throat, or carrying out a day at work. We let life pass without actually living it. Then we complain of the missing zest and vibrancy in our lives — the joie de vivre.

"If you are depressed, you are living in the past. If you are anxious, you are living in the future. If you are at peace, you are living in the present." -Lao Tzu

While oscillating between the past and the future, our mind constantly projects the vision of a perfect happy life, having the perfect life partner, all the success, a fat balance in the bank account, and so on. Anything less than this envisioned life feels like a failure. We constantly scrutinise our past and anticipate the future. These comparisons to the perfect life trickery take us to the past, feeling sorry for not doing enough or always anticipating on the plans, warding us off from living copiously in the present. We cannot deny that our mind is ceaselessly swaying in the middle of an intimidating assumption about something yet to happen or summoning up from a past one, holding us captive in them and abandoning the present. We are continuously consumed by the process of rationalisation and evaluation, drawing patterns in the way our life works.

Since the past and the future do not hold any reality in the now, aren't they mere illusions affecting your mental wellbeing? Aren't you always entangling yourself with nervous tension wrapped with regret, anger, and worry about something that can't be changed or predicted?

Even though we all are aware of the repercussions of living in the illusions of the past or the future, yet fail to focus on the present. These thoughts build up illusionary expectations, and convince the present that it's not living up to them, thus the viscous circle of wandering thoughts and suffering continues. The disharmony between thoughts and reality creates instability in life, diminishing one's capacity to be happy or content.

A famous dictum says that if the body is in the present moment, so should your thoughts be.

Living in the present is living with the acknowledgment of what is, and accepting it as it is without prejudice. If you get anxious about what might be and what might have been, you will lose on enjoying what is. Don't give up on your life, for everything is complete as it is. Bend your reality, your time and place, to align it with the present. Choose your actions while feeling them consciously in that time. Shift your focus from everything else to the action in sight, and engage in it as if it is the only thing that exists in that moment. Drive out scepticism, disbelief, dullness and interferences, and centre yourself to the chosen task. Do not indulge in the thoughts of how a new venture will measure up on the success graph, just focus on what needs to be done in the moment. Plan and set goals, but accept and acknowledge each moment as it unfolds.

When you choose to live in the now, you indubitably let go of the bygone events and anticipation of the future. It does not imply that you have no dreams or goals in life. Think of it as the moment of doing. We all have moments when we fear what's to come or what may be. We all have desires and ambitions in life, but we are so bogged down with the little things that we overlook the bigger goal, and when we focus on the bigger dreams, we fail to rejoice in the pleasures of the small things in life. Sometimes, we do things because we simply want to, while at other times we give reasons for not doing them. Whenever you feel stuck, simply make up your mind whether you want to go ahead and do something or not. Don't let your mind linger over it. Take action, live the experience, whether good or bad, then let it pass. Remember to live each moment, seize each opportunity and embrace your life.

Mystical Hues

Sometimes there…sometimes a pass...
Instinctively knocking in a brisk...
Years may pass and then a moment will click...
For the purpose is calling...
For the sun is shining...
Clear the conscience and the long poignant dues...
Oh, these mystical hues...

- PaYal Jain

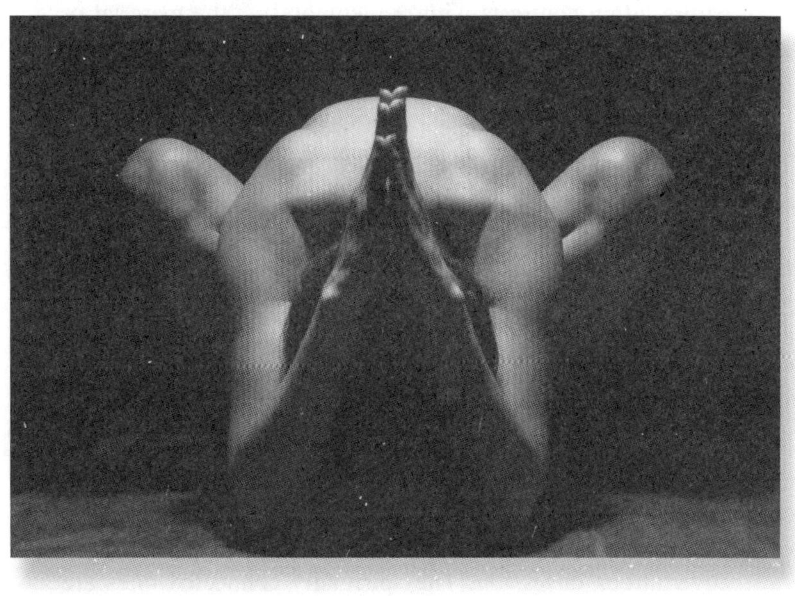

The Connect Within

Spirituality, in a narrow sense, concerns itself with matters of the spirit. The spiritual, involving (as it may) perceived eternal verities of humankind's ultimate nature, often contrasts with the temporal — the material or the worldly. A sense of connection forms the central defining characteristic of spirituality–connection with something greater than oneself, which includes an emotional experience of religious awe and reverence. Equally important is spirituality's relation to matters of sanity and psychological health. Like some forms of religion, spirituality often focuses on personal experience. Spirituality may involve perceiving life on a higher plane, more complex or integrated with one's world view, as opposed to merely sensual.

We humans are held captive by the matrix of materialistic influences and dwell in those stimuli while putting ourselves far away from our own spirituality. Spirituality is a way of life or a state of mind. It goes beyond attending a spiritual workshop or having a goal to achieve, or complying with the worldly definitions that craft the spiritual quest like an adventurous obsession. The spiritually connected ones are so present in the moment, crazy curious, and are completely passionate about anything and everything they are involved with. We are spiritually connected as children. That's the time when we are absorbing, learning and forever growing with wonder and admiration for all things. Spirituality is being aware of the now in unification with the world around.

As adults, we consider spirituality as an aim or goal to achieve, which fails to quench the spiritual thirst. From birth till the age of six or seven, we are in alignment with our true spiritual selves, but then our personality becomes entangled with material living, burying our spirituality under. Spirituality or 'the connect' within aids us in understanding the meaning of life and guides us towards the purpose of life. We all our born with this 'the connect', and the sensors to pick on signals that give direction to the course of life. That is the reason why somethings that we think of or anticipate come true as real manifestations. We call it gut, intuition, the sixth sense, failing to see the light of intellect and spirituality building inside us. Children have a highly activated sense in that regard.

Our sense of self keeps changing from I to us when in a relationship and expands with the family. After a while, it gets confined within certain boundaries. This sense of self does get competitive at times and jealous at others, because it is not aligned with the universe outside our expansion. When we expand our sense of self beyond our family boundaries to encompass everything, identifying the self with the universe and beyond, we truly achieve the mystic experience that merges with the material.

Running after tangible pleasures, we overlook the peace, joy, calmness, and love within. We associate our happiness with these material possessions, but there is no end to them so they fail to maintain our happiness and contentment. Thus, the quest never ends. You may climb the tallest mountain, or cross the seven seas, earn in figures you can't count or be the most powerful or the most famous; underneath it all lies the longing to just be happy.

We seldom feel content with what we have. How many times have you had sex without getting conscious of your own body or performance? How many times do you register the real taste of food while eating your everyday meal? Slowing down and walking towards spirituality leads you to start living. Pursuing the mystical path entails giving your mind a respite from running after material happiness.

Spirituality holds a different meaning for each and every person; not confirming to any fixated ideology. Each one of us is unique, a different soul driven by a different mystically. So is the spiritual journey where all the ways leads to living each moment and improving every day through self-introspection. If you are continuously ameliorating, becoming a better person than you were yesterday, then you are growing spiritually. It does take effort to be one with the paradoxes of the spiritual path while willing to let it all go on the path of truth where all obstacles and possibilities come under equivalence. Spirituality will not make all your worries vanish, but it will bring your conscience to peace and present you with the truth, for you are the knowledge, the knowing and the knower.

In an instantaneous moment, a sudden sense surges, outpouring emotions that immerse your whole existence. What prompts these flashes of feelings could be anything from a major occurrence in life to weeping induced by a movie scene. These feelings my change your perspective of the world and connect you with your spiritual side. When this unification with the self is made, one manages to break the chains of materialism and embark upon an inexplicable mystical process that brings in awareness. A seeker is then born that lives life authentically while opening the self to the pathway of transformation. Our mystical self then comes in contact with the pedestal of the soul, and becomes one with the light of inner beauty. The moment we know and acknowledge who we are in alignment with the universe; we begin to be spiritually connected. We gather the courage in these moments to look inwards and hear the inner voice, same as the voice of God.

Let Forgiveness Seep In

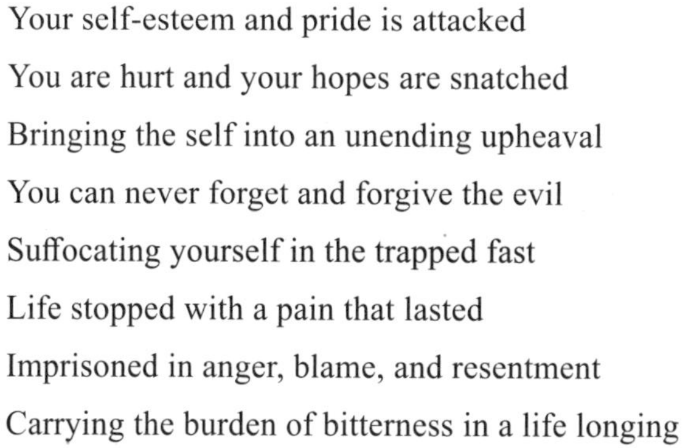

Your self-esteem and pride is attacked
You are hurt and your hopes are snatched
Bringing the self into an unending upheaval
You can never forget and forgive the evil
Suffocating yourself in the trapped fast
Life stopped with a pain that lasted
Imprisoned in anger, blame, and resentment
Carrying the burden of bitterness in a life longing impairment
Owing the righteous rage, you reject and criticise
Consumed by pride, you continue to suffer inside
Explanations get in the way of forgiveness
Filling you with a blank impassive stiffness
Buried under the pile of self-pity and fury
Scars playing your judge and the jury
Lived the pain time and again in the verdict
Suffocated in the reality and revocation conflict
Dwelled in sorrow while building coping strategies
Submerging deeper in the past anatomies
Longing to free the self from incessant pain

While being chained in vengeance over and over again
Darkness tangling through self-doubt into eternity
Allow the light to let in healing certainty
Rise over the pain and let it stay where it belonged
Accept it as it happened, not making right the wrong
It is time to close the doors behind
Take the lessons and live with this new find
Letting go of our anger, allowing forgiveness to seep in
Freeing yourself of the shackles, mending within
Free yourself of the agony once and for all
You must go onward and live life as it calls

- PaYal Jain

The Forgiving Intricacy

Your boss drives you nuts and leaves no opportunity to insult you in front of all your colleagues. Your father controls every aspect of your life. Your in-laws make your life hell in all possible ways. A stranger hurts you bad and leaves you with a lifelong impairment. Your spouse humiliates you in front of your friends and relatives, and no one even defends you. Your boyfriend/girlfriend cheats on you. Your best friend walks out of your life without an explanation. You ingratiate yourself with hatred towards the uncle who sexually abused you. Your father abuses you and your mother doesn't utter a word against it.

Life present us certain situations where we get hurt and it leaves unending upheavals in our hearts. We feel betrayed, offended, wounded and wronged, accumulating resentments. Forgiving is out of question, for the hurt caused remains with most of us forever. It is a survival impulse for us to not forgive, fearing a repeat of this hurt. After any kind of injury, our hopes become threadbare and we choose to stay on guard in response. We stack up piles of rage and fury and maintain this shield. We foster coping strategies that include becoming emotionless and cold hearted, dismissive, forgetful, distanced, indulging in revengeful actions, etc. in terms with the wrath and rage causing a turmoil inside us.

If forgiving a person who caused you immeasurable hurt is making you feel perturbed and uneasy, it is okay and normal. Our evolution as a race has taught us to not accept exploitation, and the simplest way to deal with it is to retaliate. When our pride has been attacked, our self-esteem has been damaged, our hope has been snatched away, we resist forgiving so as to counterweigh the hurt. 'I am the one dealing with the consequences of the hurt, so I will not forgive', 'I will forgive only if he acts in a certain manner', 'I refuse to reconcile the relationship so I won't forgive'. Many such explanations will get in the way of forgiveness.

Forgiveness does not imply forgetting. We must not ever forget the painful experience of getting hurt, but accept that it has happened and nothing in the entire universe holds the power to revoke the same. These uncomfortable experiences will be a part of your life till the very end, churning anger and resentment inside you, and controlling your very existence. It is only when you forgive that you free yourself of the control of these emotions as well as the experience of those dreadful events.

We often believe that forgiving is a trait of the weak, and refuse to be part of that ignominious lot. Wearing the cape of toughness, we freeze these resentments, feel bitter and revengeful with a sustained feeling of self-righteousness. We push away feelings of hurt with self-pity, fury and vengeance while saving ourselves from facing our vulnerabilities. Our rejection for amnesty then becomes a permanent fragment of our being and we get hemmed in with our perpetual misery. We focus more on the happening itself, the unfairness and cruelty, than our reaction to it. Inadvertently, we continue to live in the past and carry on that pain into the present, allowing it to hurt us over and over again.

When we choose to be in the chains of emotional hurt from the past and refuse to forgive, we get stuck living with the burden of bitterness. Forgiveness is not strictly a reconciliation, but it gives you the opportunity and power to define the stance of the relationship in the future.

Forgiveness is for the inner self; it is about the acceptance of what happened and retrieving oneself from the cage of the past, of the resentment which otherwise will tear down many aspects of our life. Things like rape and murder are completely unacceptable, but if we allow ourselves to understand the sociology and psychology behind these acts, we begin to be a part of the formation process leading to a crime free world. By forgiving, we allow ourselves to act out of knowledge rather than impulse.

As long as we do not forgive we hurt ourselves with the callousness nurturing the resentment by living in the incident of the past. We are always the victims suppressing the forgiveness and withhold ourselves from feeling anything beyond the past injuries of life, being hurt and betrayed by everyone in the present taking no responsibility for it or so. Frightened and terrified, we fail to accept and confront ourselves as we are and therefore cast these offensive projections onto others, deceiving ourselves for what is acceptable or unacceptable. Projecting our flaws onto others has been ingrained in us since generations. Our parents had their own flaws and their parents had their own and they passed on these inadequacies making us feel responsible for their unacceptable parts, for their misery in some ways or the other. Look around and you will see ample validations in politics, self-righteous groups, movies, journalism, etc. pervasively creating the other as the villain and the self as the victim.

True strength is seen when there is a shift from the victim stance and one recognises the ability to forgive. We forgive ourselves many times and in many ways, so this ability is deep seated within us. No one in this world has a perfect life or has not made any mistakes. As humans, we sometimes ill-treat one another, intentionally and unintentionally. Think of the times when you were on the other side and sought forgiveness. Jesus underwent immense pain, indignity and humiliation and when he was being crucified, he asked God to forgive the people who were killing him. Despite living a sinless life, he paid the penalty for all of humankind's sin and died on the cross.

Progressing toward a forgiving attitude can take years of self-work and courage to deal with the damaged self. Even if your scars run really deep, forgiving is worth everything. It will not undo the event, but will free you of the pain.

"When a deep injury is done to us, we never heal until we forgive."

–Nelson Mandela

Grateful

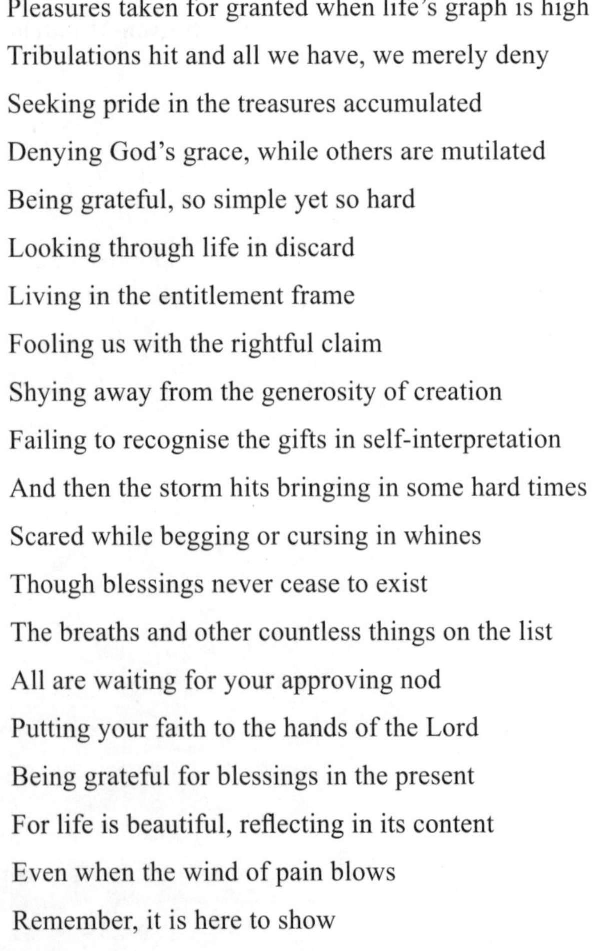

Pleasures taken for granted when life's graph is high
Tribulations hit and all we have, we merely deny
Seeking pride in the treasures accumulated
Denying God's grace, while others are mutilated
Being grateful, so simple yet so hard
Looking through life in discard
Living in the entitlement frame
Fooling us with the rightful claim
Shying away from the generosity of creation
Failing to recognise the gifts in self-interpretation
And then the storm hits bringing in some hard times
Scared while begging or cursing in whines
Though blessings never cease to exist
The breaths and other countless things on the list
All are waiting for your approving nod
Putting your faith to the hands of the Lord
Being grateful for blessings in the present
For life is beautiful, reflecting in its content
Even when the wind of pain blows
Remember, it is here to show

These are just lessons to unfold
To complete the life you hold
Remember each thing, big or small
Raising you high and making you fall
It is meant to make you grow by all means
So be grateful for all of life's sheen

- PaYal Jain

intrepid
radiant
visionary
artistic
daring
delighted
aspiring
ingenious
grateful
fluid
inventive
wondrous
thankful
appreciative
clever
artistic
inspired
daring
joyful
beautiful
resourceful
imaginative
visionary
beautiful
imaginative
creative
radiant
inspired
fluid
clever
wondrous
grateful
joyful
dynamic
creative
thankful
creative
adventurous

Coming Out of the Entitlement Frame

When we are happy, we have so many things to be grateful for and so many reasons to thank life, thank God and thank almost everyone, but the same becomes a challenging task when life is a little rough on the graphs. When the going gets tough and everything is haywire, we fall to frustrations and gloominess, blaming situations and self-pitying. Have you ever met someone who has all rosy days in his/her life? All of us have some low times in our lives at some point or the other and when the lows hit, we tend to forget all the highs and curse our luck and belittle all our blessings. We get into the loop of constant complaining even when most of our life is convenient. Stress and criticism becomes our second nature and then comes along annoyance, disappointment and hollowness. We tend to neglect so many things, including our health, our relationships, etc. and start taking them for granted. We fall prey to the delusion of permanence and believe that they will last forever.

We are living in a world where everyone is compensating for happiness by accumulating materialistic belongings. We have accumulated wealth and power and take all the pride in the achievement while making a fool of ourselves by attributing everything to our efforts alone. Seen through the lens of only entitlement, we fail to express gratitude as if the universe owes us all that we have. Living in this frame of mind, we practice ingratitude and become a bee in our bonnet, closing our eyes to all those who helped us directly or indirectly.

When everything is great, we overlook the gratitude and when everything is in turmoil and life seems to suck, we find it extremely difficult to come across things we are grateful for. Paradoxically, practicing gratitude is so simple and yet so hard to actually put into practice. We are just so fixated on seeing the bad that we forget that the good even exists. Even in the darkest hours, there is always something to feel gratitude for: a sunny day after a week of bone chilling winter days, the smiles of your children playing outdoors, the fact that you have all the organs of your body in place and so on. Gratitude takes us through our true riches and clarity prevails, giving us a new perspective on the goals we pursue, our relationships, and other things aligning with the values and the intentions we hold in our lives.

In a study conducted on gratitude, it was found that people who practice gratitude on an everyday basis have higher levels of attentiveness, awareness, fortitude, zeal, positivity and vigour. They also display strength of mind and character in dealing with life's lows. They are more willing to reach out and help, push their limits towards personal goals, tend to be more creative and more resilient. They have a healthy body and a strong immune system. It was also found that these people have happier and stronger relationship bonds than those who don't practice gratitude. Gratitude precipitates consideration and this thoughtfulness nurtures relationships. When we practice gratitude, we identify that all of us have some bad days and the rumination of their bad mood is not the reflection of their true feelings. We become more grateful towards loved ones even after the honeymoon phase is over for we are glad for the things that the other person does right and not fall into the trap of constantly chiming about the wrongs.

'Rise and go; your faith has made you well.' (Luke 17: 16 -18)

In the passage from the New Testament gospel of Luke, Jesus meant thankfulness by 'faith', and also hinted at the forgetfulness by which most pick on ingratitude. Gratitude is acknowledging the giftedness and generosity of the creation. Alternately, ingratitude is living in denial of the giftedness. When we live with gratitude, we know that life is a gift. We know that we are able to see the beautiful skies because of the gift of sight. My spouse, my children, the food on my plate, every breath I take is a gift. The true fortune lies in your experiences of small pleasures of the present moment. Of the ten Jesus healed, only one recognised the giftedness, the fortune, and expressed gratitude, while the nine did not, but Jesus did not ask them to return and express the same.

Gratitude takes away your focus from the negative. Even when things take a wrong turn, gratitude knows that eventually something substantial will breed out of the rough going through. It is living life in a new way by which things are seen in a state of sheer positivity. Gratitude is a choice and the key to true happiness. Being grateful is not putting on rose-coloured glasses forever, but to ascertaining the value of things in your life that bring the smallest or grandest delight. It also means taking cognizance of the blessings which are taken for granted otherwise, and eventually gaining an emotional balance. Once gratitude has found a profound place in your life, you will also feel connected within and with the outside world. When you notice and acknowledge an act of kindness coming from someone, you will feel elated of your belonging to a caring world.

Not all in the world are fortunate enough to clothe their bodies, have food on their plate or rooftop over their heads, while those who have them overlook them until intimidated with its confiscation. Instead of feeling grateful for what we have, we fall into the trap of comparison, wishing a better lifestyle, a bigger house, a bigger car, more travel, we become obsessed with endless wants and desires of what is missing in life and actually miss out on what we already have. Pause this moment and mull over all the gratifying things in your life. Be thankful for all the times that did not go wrong and all the lessons you learnt from the times that did. Nothing stays permanent in life and things we rightfully claim to be ours can be snatched away in a split second. Take a moment to be thankful for having experienced them; acknowledge the blessings in your lives. Notice just how many you failed to recognise earlier, lost sight by simply taking them for granted. Embrace this moment in gratitude, admiring and appreciating all that you have and yes. life is beautiful.

Be grateful for all you have and all you don't, for now there is something to look for,

Be grateful for all you know and all you don't, for there is something to learn,

Be grateful for the good times and all the lows, for there is something that will make you grow,

Be grateful for your strengths and your weaknesses, for there is something to build upon,

Be grateful for all the light and dark in your life, for there is a meaning to seek,

Be grateful for the breaths taken, for there is yet life to witness

With love, admiration and thankfulness.

To All The Soulmates

To all those who crossed my path
No matter whether they brought along smiles or wrath
For changing my life in ways, big or small
For fitting in just right, like the missing piece balancing in all
To all those who stayed for whatever time they could
And the strangers whom I completely misunderstood
For making me look into the parts I denied
For completing me through the churn inside
To all those who hurt me, stretching my limits
And paying me those annoying visits
For abetting me to respond right
For teaching me when to stay mum and when to fight
To all those who saw through me
Destined like always meant to be
For coming and going out of my life
For amplifying my growth like a guide
To all those who left imprints on my heart
Did not realise till they did depart
It felt as if they took a piece when they left

In reality, it completed me just the way it was meant to
To all my lost and found soulmates
Those who let me crash into their heart's gates
We were fated to complete each other in certain ways
For steering together through life's maze

- PaYal Jain

Thank You For Crossing My Path

In this one life of ours, many cross our path and become our destiny in some way. Their impact on us becomes an inseparable part of our lives that stays with us forever. These include family, friends, associates, and neighbours, strangers who smiled or made up raise our brow or changed us in some way. There are many whom we meet in our lives and they shape us in some manner or the other. You might have interacted with some, while all those who stayed for a longer time have an incalculable impact on your life, yet they are shown contempt for.

Looking at your life retrospectively, the many people whom you have encountered are your soul mates, whether the encounter with them has been at a personal level or not. They were there for a reason, for the impact, for broadening your experience of yourself and to bring you in contact with unconditional love, and acceptance. These are the people who make you feel as good and beautiful as the concept of soulmates in our heads, and these are also the people who will make you feel damaged. These are the people who are able to see your soul, unveil you layer by layer till you get to see your naked-self, terrifying you at times, making you confront your fears, breaking your heart but also leading you to be courageous to break down your own walls.

We often confuse the meaning of a soulmate with 'the one'. Most of us believe the cliché paradigm related to there being only one person in life, as in all the romantic movies, that is meant to complete you in all possible ways; that one special person we will fall in love with forever and live happily ever after. If one person was enough to complete you in all ways, why is our life affected by many? People bump into your life for your growth which could come along with happiness, contentment, or even triggering a turmoil within you, leading to a feeling of completeness. If you experienced or provided opportunities of growth to/from certain people, it is likely that you had some soul connection with them. Not all relationships are meant to be rosy, neither are they meant to be exigent all the time, but all of them teach us something, perhaps a new aspect of ourselves. You will cherish and acknowledge these soulmates from time to time, recalling the beautiful mystery of the rendezvous. All these are meant to show up in your life for particular periods of time for reasons that may make no sense at that time, but make perfect sense later.

I recall one very brief meeting with a stranger that changed my perspective on judgements forever. I was wandering at the railway platform waiting for my delayed train while killing time and burning calories. While I was strolling, this seven or eight year old boy drew my attention as he was wearing some fifteen to eighteen earrings and was looking quite a weirdo. His appearance was bit kooky and bizarre that made me judge the parents' decision of letting their child not only look freaky, but also letting him go through the pain for their own vogue desires. I could not hold myself from drawing the attention of my husband to him. The child's mother overheard my comments and walked up to me. I felt embarrassed, but the moment of truth soon arrived. She told me that she had lost five of her children before him right after giving them birth and some person told them that if these holes were pierced in the new-born's ear with specific earrings, the child will survive. They had done what they were asked to do, and their son was alive, smiling and playing in front of them. Regardless of the fact whether I believed in the superstition or not, I did realise the intensity of hurt my comment must have caused her. That was the day I realised that at times we just judge people without knowing what they have gone through, and it often brings back so much pain, like I brought back the pain of her dead children. I never met her in my life again, but the lesson stayed, leaving a big impact on me. I realised that day that we have to trust and embrace the coming and going of these soulmates as the mysterious reason for them being there will unfold in time.

These strong encounters become an integral part of our being. Have you ever felt a certain draw towards a person, and sometimes a dislike without an explanation towards a particular person? Usually, you will have some sense of understanding when meeting these individuals for the first time. You bump into any person for a reason and the people who do cross the path of your life are like your extended entity. A soulmate can also be seen as a person who reflects us in some way. These souls remind us of our known and unknown selves.

Instant attraction or repulsion is defined by the extent of connectedness we feel with someone, and science is now exploring the connection we feel with people. There is a scientific clarification that explains feeling connected with some and disconnected with others. In one of the studies in this field, it is stated that 'As the heart beats, it generates a large electromagnetic field which radiates externally to the body, and is literally a measurable magnetic field.' We all have had moments where we felt an instant attraction or the absence of it. Have you ever felt a change in the frequency of connectedness within the same conversation with the same person? This happens because the electromagnetic fields change, and so do the relationships in our lives.

The bond shared with each of our soulmates is truly exceptional, and each of these connections complements a distinct attribute of us. No matter how separated the soulmates are by time or distance, there will bc a connectedness the moment you are united, like picking up from where you last left off. Meeting them is like meeting a missing part of us, whether we are aware of it then or not. To all my parts, some I have met and some are still yet to cross my path, I want to say that I am thankful to you for being there in my life. No matter how we affect each other's life, whether in a big way or small, I am glad we crossed each other's path and be fortunate enough to have the understanding of that connection.

The Treasure You Have

What is it that you really own?

What wealth of yours can be shown?

What all do you claim as 'mine'?

What legacy will you leave behind?

What wealth of yours can't be stolen away or destroyed?

What riches of the treasures can't be toyed?

Are you wealthy with treasures of wisdom and understanding?

Are you increasing your wealth while experiencing expansion?

Are you feeling abundant while enjoying simplicity in life?

Are you building wealth free of the fake and real strife?

Are you creating wealth by creating value no price tag can match?

Are you securing wealth that no entity can ever detach?

Counting on your worldly possessions

You come across your wealth confessions,

None to accompany when you leave empty handed

Your treasures to leave you dejected and stranded,

Only karma to carry forward and impact to leave after

The tears you begot or the spread laughter,
The values, the character or the skills you profess
Make you wealthy and not what you thought less,
Having a home with a family that bonds over love
Is truly a blessing, a treasure far above,
No pleasure in the brands and status chase
The ability to affect and embrace,
True wealth is looking at life with blessing shutters
While you endorse a meaning to life, for self and for others.

- PaYal Jain

True Wealth

What is it that you have? Whenever we have to answer that question, we start counting the materialistic wealth we have acquired, or at least the immediate thoughts go towards the possessions. It is strange that all our lives we claim to have so much, yet leave this world empty-handed, just the way we had arrived. No one takes with him the lavish house, the fancy car, or the money in the bank, for they are all left for the family. The rich, the poor, the powerful or the weak, all will leave the world the same way as the body. No material wealth, nothing claimed as 'mine' accompanies one to the deathbed, but only karma to take over and the impact one left behind will be the wealth that one carries forward.

There are many tales about King Alexander's last wishes, though there aren't any strong historical references to the same. Whether these tales hold true or not, they truly hint at the wealth metaphor. According to these legends, King Alexander was once returning home after conquering most of the world's empires and their wealth when he fell ill and realised that his death was near. He asked his men to carry out his three wishes after his departure, which were:

1. His coffin would be carried by his physicians alone.

2. The path on which his coffin was to be carried towards the graveyard should be scattered with the treasures he had collected.

3. His hands should be left hanging from the coffin.

The tale hints that Alexander realised that it was not his true wealth. Through these wishes, he wanted the world to not take health for granted, for no best doctors in the world can cure you when it is the time to go. He wanted to see his mother, but his health did not allow it and none of his physicians could help him do so for they were all powerless. The second wish explains that no treasure goes with you, no matter how much time, effort you invested in chasing it. Not even a portion of the pots of wealth Alexander collected could go with him. About his hands, he wanted to convey that you come empty handed and shall leave empty handed too.

Alexander is remembered for his great battle skills, and is also seen as power hungry who conquered most of the world. That's how Alexander lived and forever will live by the legacy he left behind. The legacy or the worth cannot be valued in materialistic terms. That is what you truly have — what you can give or share and leave an impact by is your true wealth, what you actually have. Can you put a price tag on Nelson Mandela's or Mother Teresa's contribution to humanity? Do you think one can come up with an amount for Mark Zukerberg's technical thinking skills and buy the same? The skills you develop over the years, the values that you draw and the character that you build are invaluable, your true wealth.

No doubt, Amitabh Bachchan makes an earning out of his acting skills, Mark Zukerberg has recognition and wealth because of his technical creative skills, and there are many others who have made a fortune from their talents, but they significantly derive fulfilment in life because of these skills, values and character. The way you exist becomes your true wealth. We must strive for a wealthy life in its truest sense, through our existence in love and relationship, by taking care of our health, by being spiritually connected and living in fulfilment, and by reminding ourselves time and again to be aligned with the skills, values and character.

When we say we come empty handed and we leave empty handed, it implies that we neither come with any of the materialistic objects that fall in the worldly definition of wealth, nor do we leave with them. We forget our true wealth, failing to acknowledge the same, for we get trapped in selfish accumulations, promoting suffering for ourselves and others. These possessions starts to shadow us, bringing us down and making us lose our sense of true wealth. We get in the rat race, accumulating more and more with no end in sight, but how many times is the intent to create value? Steve Jobs, Oprah Winfrey, and many others created value for whatever they did for they gave themselves the chance to reach out to their true wealth: their soul.

Your wisdom and judgement are things that no one can snatch away. The love of learning or finding joy in the simple pleasures of life, being content and grateful for abundance in life are the things you will never be able to buy. True wealth is having a home with a close bond of love and belonging to a family, and not a house of a desired size. True wealth is not acquiring the comforts that make life easy, but sharing those comforts with others too, for that will be appreciation in the value of these comforts. It is not the branded clothes that makes you look wealthy, but a healthy body that fits in the clothes that matters. The smiles and support of the loved ones when the party is over is your true asset. You may buy the latest or the most expensive smart phones, but if you have no people to call in times of despair or emergency, you are surely not rich enough. If you are just living to the tunes of duties, social stigmas and responsibilities, cheating on your own soul, you deplete your true wealth. You don't get your hands on true wealth through possessions, but through experiences to endorse a meaningful life, not for the self alone, but for others too. Wealth cannot be measured in possessions, but in the ability to affect others in the most positive way and impact the world in the most constructive way. When you are about to leave the world, will you be leaving wealthy through how you existed, or will you die without existing, without creating meaning in life?

"The key to understanding if something is truly precious is to ask if we can hold it, for things truly precious cannot be held." — Craig D. Lounsbrough

A Few Moments

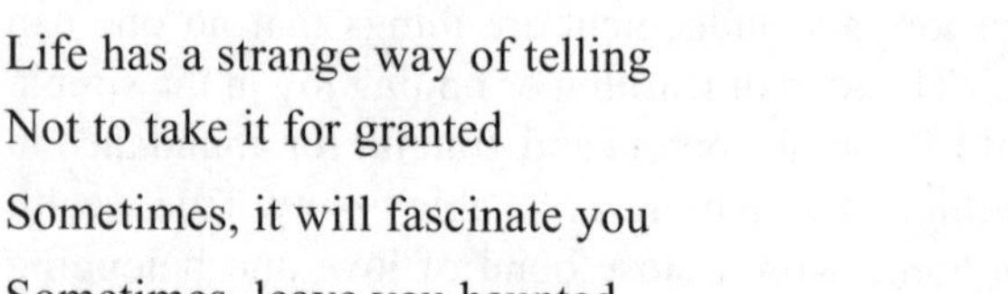

Life has a strange way of telling
Not to take it for granted
Sometimes, it will fascinate you
Sometimes, leave you haunted
You cannot escape the exit for sure
So you plead for a few moments, seeking the cure

Waiting in line to be evolved
Do you think you had it all solved?
Looking for answers one may never find
For the questions are not very clear in the mind
You cannot leave with the chaotic estimation
So you plead for a few moments, reconciling the self-relation

Regrets burying down your soul
While you failed in achieving your true goal
In attempts of making others happy, but you
Delaying the joy, dismissing the worthy due
You cannot partially go feeling incomplete
So you plead for a few moments to erase the deceit

You do not say ‘sorry’ or ‘love you’ when you should
While your inner feelings were mostly misunderstood
You did not make your dreams come true
And did not live authenticating the real you
You do not miss what life was always flashing
So you plead for a few moments and catch up with what life was snatching.

- PaYal Jain

Grant Me A Few Moments More

While we are waiting in the queue, we reminisce and ruminate over the flashes we will see when it shall be the time to leave, the last things that will weigh on our minds just before we simply stop existing. We often hear that when it is time to go, life will flash in front of your eyes while you are fading away with these scenes, and plenty of cogitations wishing for some more moments to finish so much more. You want a few moments more, for there was a plan for how your life was supposed to shape; triumphs all along the journey with no room for errors. And now, death is about to make the final move and the plot of our achievements and our life is ready to be thrashed. Dying is inevitable, yet when you hear these distant sirens, you are gloomed with darkness, asking for a few moments more to live a life that felt true to you, to take that music course over that engineering degree, to undo the bad choices you made or the good ones you did not make, to have lived for happiness and not have chased after the never ending materialistic treasures. How you wish to have been granted just a few moments more, to have lived before you are ready to go.

When we look back on how most of us lived our life, we see the commonality in not being authentic to our true thoughts, with no harmony in what we said, felt or did, living a lie.

हसीं में अक्सर गम छिपाए बैठे है ,
परतों में दिल के अहसास दबाए बैठे है,
अहसासों में शक के ताले लगाए बैठे है,
रूठे है खुद से और ज़माने मनाये बैठे है |

–पायल जैन

Smiling through hidden layers of despair

True emotions enclosed in curtains over the heart

Locking our own thoughts with doubts

Nettled with the self, yet making everyone happy, falsely reaching out…

Life is so uncertain and unpredictable, and the only thing that is certain is the uncertainty of life slipping away. Are we living in lies only to regret it when all of a sudden we have to leave, longing for a few moments more to live authentically for once before it is time go? Why are we living while controlling, when we know this remote can be snatched away by ambiguity and unpredictability at any given point of time? Why are we begging for time to voice and act out our buried feelings when we have had a lifetime to do so? And now we ask for a few moments more to work on the strengthening of relationships than the bank balance, to have taken time to love and express, to have stayed in touch with people that mattered. Many live on by postponing their happiness to the day that might never come, and then ask to be granted a few moments more on that one day.

We all are aware of our limited time here, yet we choose to deny our happiness and invest our energies in things away from a happy and fulfilled life. No matter what roles we play in our lives, we are constantly worrying and living in fear to live up to the expectations of others. As parents, as a junior worker in a company or the CEO, as the famous or the commoner, we all are worrying ourselves up with something or the other and allowing this heaviness to slog us down. We overlook the joys of the roles we are in, while the worry takes over most of the moments from these roles. And when the time is near, how we wish to be granted a few moments more to enjoy the role we played on the stage of life or to discover the role for us. Many just carried on the assigned roles, not looking for their own, suppressing their feelings, settling for a mediocre life instead of what they truly could be.

Some may never experience these intense feelings for they are living life to the fullest or they are living in full and sure claims of prophecy of their lives. But whenever and whosoever has experienced that intense feeling of life going by way too fast is looking for this grant of a few moments more, for they are just discovering the purpose that is meant to make them feel alive now. Why do we need wake up calls most times, like an emergency open-heart surgery, or the news that my time is near and no medicine can help me extend my stay and grant me the time I need.

Most of us don't want to die. Not because of the repentant and remorseful feelings for what they had done or had not done, but because there is so much more they could be feeling, as it does not feel complete to go. When death is knocking at your door, are you ready to leave or are you pleading him to grant a few moments more?

To have these moments granted would always be an illusion, but imagine what it would be like if you could be granted these moments to reconnect with the very core of who you really are, and what truly matters to you? Will you bring to an end the vicious circle of pleasing others and delaying living your life to the truest? Will you rekindle and reignite your relationships with more meaning and purpose? Will you say your "I love you" and "I'm sorry" and forgive those who needs to be forgiven?

Remember, your time is limited and use each moment to let go of all the outer expectations, all egotism, all embarrassment of failure and truly follow your heart. Life does not only flash before you when it is time to go, life has been flashing forever since the day we were born. Life always served choices flashing right in front of us, but we did not take the path or explored our chances, hoping and longing for a few moments more.

"It's only when we truly know and understand that we have a limited time on Earth–and that we have no way of knowing when our time is up–that we will begin to live each day to the fullest, as if it was the only one we had."

- Elisabeth Kubler-Ross

The Forgotten Fossil

Disillusioned, dejected, discarded, disowned, disgraced by
Friends and foes, kith and kin
And then the fatal blow, the blatant betrayal
Your own flesh and blood,
The one closest to your heart
From this one you can never arise
From now, you are nothing but a forgotten fossil
Fearing this moment since forever
Finding ways to give the existence a meaning
Helpless in doing anything about dying
Counting on the left legacy
Feared life all the while, fearing death now
From this moment, extinction may follow
From now, you are nothing but a forgotten fossil
Ready or not, death will knock at your door
Leaving you with no choice but to answer
Separating you from everything you claimed to be yours
For no one will accompany you to the unknown realm
Hurt with the parting and the disconnection
From this realisation, loneliness creeps in

From now, you are nothing but a forgotten fossil
Unprepared, scared you gather your courage
To face the other side, to face the unknown
And suddenly, the lost voice speaks up
There is nothing to be frightened of
Life and death will happen as they are meant to be
For you have always been a forgotten fossil
And an eternal soul learning lessons all the while…

- PaYal Jain

Glimpse Of The Other Side

We are surrounded by death in many ways and yet the existence that embodies both life and death is escaping the ultimate certainty. Death is inevitable, yet we don't accept it. Everything is over in a split second as you lie unaware of the silence, the whispers and a sense of awe. Death is the permanent form of briefness putting on view that all will pass and everything we have been living will fade away in the final moments, and we all will be nothing but a forgotten fossil. Humans fear the over and done, and to be remembered they indulge in things which will make their existence last forever. Having a family is also in that vain to leave a genetic legacy. They engage in things that will last even when they are gone including art, music, social, political movements, etc. giving meaning to their lives. Those who did not make these connections lie there in delusion, dejection, disgraced while disowned to their own meanings of life. Death is meaningful in itself for it tests the meaning of life. Life's final meaning stays uncertain until we are betrayed by our own flesh and blood and it echoes through the face of death.

"The fear of death follows from the fear of life. A man who lives fully is prepared to die at any time."–Mark Twain

Ready or not, one day death will come knocking and one has to answer the door. Your fortunes, fame and clout will be all irrelevant. Even your own body, the gender or the colour of your skin, will all be immaterial. Nothing will matter but the acts of truthfulness, candour, kind-heartedness, and courage that deepened your existence and of others while empowering and encouraging others through your actuality in the cycle of life and death. Most die without even living, for they had no clue about how to live, they just carried out what the society coerced. Frightened they live and freighted they die. The man who lived fearlessly and faced the uncertainties with equality, life and death became the same for him as there was no conflict or fear.

Death is all around, giving signs of its existence. We attend funerals of people who were once laughing and crying with us before they bid their final goodbyes. Everything will fade away eventually, be it the leaves turning yellow from green and then falling off to be brushed away. When we look at these leaves, these lifeless trees, we are not dismayed for their withering; for the law of their fading is the very law of their new emergence. A lot has been said by believers on how you would be reunited with lost loved ones in a heavenly place when the fatal siren blows, or non-believers who believe it to be the end and nothing happens once you have passed away, death still remains as one of life's greatest mysteries.

Dying with regrets is a common phenomenon with most of the humans, for they don't create meaning to life. When we opt for denial, we are becoming a slave to the fear of death compelling ignorance. Death is frightening for most of us, but denying it will bring about nothing, filled with pitiful hollowness. We are billions and trillions in number living on this earth, belonging to different regions and cultures and despite having some alike values, there are no two persons on this entire planet who are exactly the same. Few of these do manage to create a legacy to be remembered forever, and the rest lie feeble, soon to be forgotten by kith and kin or friends and foes. No matter which side we be on, one common thing we will have with all who exist or have ever existed or will ever come into existence is bing delivered from a mother's womb at the time of birth, and secondly to face death.

Death anxiety is a common thing and if you think of it, it is the assumption of the unknown that creates fear. Death calls to mind fears of parting and separation, hurt, pain, suffering and anxiety and so much more. As long as the assumed image exists, so will be the fear and resistance against the inevitable. When we refuse to accept the inevitable, we detach living from dying and bring fear into existence. Most of us are frightened of dying because we don't know what it means to live. Most of the human race is just struggling to get through the day, but this 'fear of the unknown' once again creeps in. We prefer to cling to the struggling known than face the unknown; the known being with a family, house, knowledge, achievements, fame, faith and every little thing that goes on endlessly till the disillusioned existence ceases. We accept the known with all its agony and despair, and get so used to it that 'the fear of the unknown' comes knocking ready to take us to a place with undefined realms.

Death, like birth, is a process where you are struggling to cling to the known while heading to something that seems to be a celestial transfer. You will be thrashing about with dejection for leaving the known, while the physical affect makes us completely unconscious to the known as we move to the unknown. Whether or not we cry and announce our arrival like we did at the time of birth is still unknown and the ones who have had near death experiences say that a bright, warm, welcoming light waits on the other side of the unknown. Death haunts us all in some way or the other with varied intensities. We tend to forget about it, being tied down to the daily routines of life, but eventually when we are taken to the world of the unknown, we will feel unnerved, panicky and confused because we would not feel prepared for it, just like we did not feel prepared at our own birth. We all have been there, taken the path leading from the known to the unknown, handling it in our own way, at our own pace, and confirmed our strengths with our first lesson and the last one. Death, like birth, is never early or late, it is just when it is meant to be.

"Just around the time when we were being born, we thought we were dying. Now we have the knowledge of birth and that there is nothing to be frightened of, as the unknown is just a change. When your time comes, you shall walk through the last mystery of life from the known to the unknown. While you walk the thin line between the known and the unknown, your soul will already have had a glimpse of the other side."

"I came with nothing and I will go with nothing but whatever I am during my time here is what simply gives meaning to my life through my lessons."

– **PaYal**

About The Author

Payal is a passionate person with feet grounded and head held high, believing that anything is possible. Having achieved feats of success in varied fields ranging from content and social media management, event management, designing curriculum and running a play-way school, inadvertently being introduced to journalism and then being a role model to many in the same, writing poetry and blogs out of passion to taking breaks for different studies in between, she followed her heart and did it all. After studying mind sciences, she was certified as an NLP and Leadership, Wellness and Executive Coach, and also practice Reiki and hypnotherapy at clinical level. She helps her clients break away from the monotony of being stuck in an undesired situation, and re-balance the various aspects of life.

f @LifeCoachPaYalJain   @life.coach.payal.jain

www.lifecoachpayaljain.com

Share your thoughts about the book using #mindlifeandreflections